NORTHEAST FOUNDATION FOR CHILDREN

D1429661

Responsive School Discipline

Essentials FOR *Elementary School Leaders*

✦

CHIP WOOD   ✦   BABS FREEMAN-LOFTIS

All net proceeds from the sale of this book support the work of Northeast Foundation for Children (NEFC). NEFC, a not-for-profit educational organization, is the developer of the *Responsive Classroom*® approach to teaching, which fosters safe, challenging, and joyful elementary classrooms and schools.

The stories in this book are all based on real events in the classroom. However, to respect the privacy of students, their names and many identifying characteristics have been changed.

ISBN: 978-1-892989-43-7

Library of Congress Control Number: 2010941601

Cover and book design by Helen Merena
Photographs © Alice Proujansky, Jeff Woodward, and Peter Wrenn. All rights reserved.
Key illustrations © Lynn Zimmerman, Lucky Dog Designs. All rights reserved.

Northeast Foundation for Children, Inc.
85 Avenue A, Suite 204
P.O. Box 718
Turners Falls, MA 01376-0718

800-360-6332
www.responsiveclassroom.org

Third printing 2012

Printed on recycled paper

CONTENTS

Part 3: Positive Behavior Everywhere

How We Want School to Be

It's first thing on a Tuesday morning in early November. The fourth and fifth graders are making the transition from first bell, heading from school breakfast, morning activities, and homework centers to their classrooms. A new student, this his second day, bumps into a smaller boy toting a heavy backpack.

"Watch it, jerk!" the new student shouts angrily.

A fifth grader spins around and says to the new student, "Whoa, we don't talk like that around here. You're new here. This is Jason. I'm Carla. Be cool, we're not gonna be late."

Down the hall, Ms. Perez is walking her second grade class to PE. A student leads the line, while Ms. Perez walks at the back of the line, where she can see the whole class. The children walk quietly in single file to keep themselves and each other safe and not disturb students in the classrooms they're passing, a way of walking they've practiced since August. As they near the office, many of the children glance up at the prominent poster of their school-wide rules. Farther down the hall, as they file past the beautiful display of student self-portraits, some students gaze and smile proudly.

When two students begin kicking each other's feet and giggling, Ms. Perez calmly moves up the line and quietly but firmly reminds them, "Hallway rules," and the two students go back to walking quietly, with hands and feet to themselves. Soon the class arrives at the gym, ready for PE.

■ ■ ■

This is just a glimpse of what school is like when school discipline is working. There is a living ethic of care. Children feel safe. They know what the expectations are and want to meet them because the adults at school have helped them understand the reasons for these expectations. They know *how* to meet the expectations because the adults have taught them the necessary skills and positive behaviors. Now these behaviors have become what students expect from each other.

This book offers school leaders strategies for achieving this kind of learning environment. Such an environment is the result of work in classrooms and at the schoolwide level. In classrooms, teachers must help students articulate classroom rules, teach children how to live by those rules, and consistently respond to misbehavior in ways that restore safety and learning and preserve the dignity of the child. At the schoolwide level, school leaders must set up systems and do the leadership work that ensures that this same kind of discipline is maintained throughout the school—not just inside classrooms, but at recess, lunch, special area classes, and everywhere in between.

This book focuses on the latter—what school leaders can do to ensure positive discipline schoolwide. For in-depth information on how teachers can achieve discipline in their classrooms, see *Rules in School: Teaching Discipline in the Responsive Classroom*, 2nd edition, by Kathryn Brady, Mary Beth Forton, and Deborah Porter, Northeast Foundation for Children, 2011, available from www.responsiveclassroom.org.

The strategies presented in this book are ones that school leaders across the nation have used with success and that you can adopt or adapt in leading your school to become a place of safe, joyful learning for every child throughout every school day.

What Is *Responsive School Discipline*?

The *Responsive School Discipline* approach is a way of creating a school climate that enables optimal academic and social growth in students. Just as teachers use the discipline practices of the *Responsive Classroom* approach to support children's positive behavior and productive learning in their classrooms, school leaders use the *Responsive School Discipline* approach to ensure that positive behavior and productive learning take place throughout the school.

About the *Responsive Classroom*® Approach

Although the strategies in this book do not demand or assume that the teachers in your school are using the *Responsive Classroom* approach, the strategies will be even more effective if they are using it. For information about the *Responsive Classroom* approach, visit www.responsiveclassroom.org and see the recommended books and DVDs in Appendix D.

The goals of the *Responsive School Discipline* approach are to ensure that children:

■ Feel physically and emotionally safe in school so that they can learn at their best.

■ Develop self-discipline and the skills for working and learning cooperatively with others.

School leaders using the *Responsive School Discipline* approach achieve these goals through the following steps:

1. **Ensuring that all adults in the school have consistent behavior expectations of students.** This means planning and leading the school's articulation of a set of schoolwide rules that apply everywhere in school and that make sense to children; establishing procedures for lunchtime, recess, and dismissal that are consistent with the schoolwide rules; and providing professional development for all staff and orchestrating communications with parents so that the whole school community has a shared understanding of the school's behavior expectations.

2. **Providing staff with professional development in the teaching of positive behavior.** Discipline is about teaching, not controlling, children. School leaders can use staff meetings and other means to help staff adopt the mentality of teaching discipline and to give them concrete skills for this teaching. An important skill to help teachers develop, for example, is using interactive modeling to teach students what following the schoolwide rules looks and sounds like in the hallways, bathrooms, cafeteria, playground, and buses.

3. **Establishing schoolwide procedures for responding to misbehavior.** An important task for school leaders is to name, or lead a committee in naming, a set of steps that all adults in the school will use in responding to student misbehavior, and then provide training for all staff— teachers as well as lunch and recess and other nonteaching staff—so that all school adults know how to use the procedures. Taking these actions ensures that when children make mistakes in their behavior, they consistently experience respectful adult responses that help them restore positive behavior.

Using the *Responsive School Discipline* approach doesn't mean your school will stop seeing challenging student behaviors. It does mean that your school will have practical and positive ways to reduce the number of behavior problems. And it means that when children's behavior does go awry, the adults at your school and the children themselves will have practical strategies for getting behavior back on track.

How Does This Fit With Anti-Bullying?

Although the strategies in this book are not intended as a specific anti-bullying program, they, along with the strategies of the *Responsive Classroom* approach (visit www.responsiveclassroom.org for information), create a safe, respectful, and caring school climate and give students a baseline of social skills competency. Regardless of the specific anti-bullying program or approach your school uses, *Responsive School Discipline* and *Responsive Classroom* strategies can enhance your school's success in addressing bullying.

For example, by giving every child a voice in morning meetings, opportunities to role-play social dilemmas, and chances to talk in class discussions, we help students develop comfort in speaking up. Speaking up when they feel unsafe or when they witness bullying will then be easier. A school using *Responsive School Discipline* and *Responsive Classroom* practices is daily helping children build the mental and moral muscles that they'll need when they confront mean behavior, and thus laying the foundation for safety against bullying.

How Long Will It Take to Implement These Strategies?

How long it takes to implement the strategies presented in this book can vary widely from school to school and depend in part on how comprehensively a school chooses to reform its discipline. If you decide that your school should focus on one specific area of concern—lunchroom discipline, for example—you would need to implement fewer strategies, and you could accomplish your goals in the course of a year. If you decide to undertake comprehensive schoolwide discipline reform, however, you may need several years.

Regardless of whether you choose focused or comprehensive reform, bear in mind that the *Responsive School Discipline* approach is not a quick fix, but a deep fix. Your school will be most successful if you model patience and persistence and allow your staff time to learn and practice positive discipline techniques meaningfully.

Also allow students time. Children don't learn and use positive behavior skills overnight any more than they do their times tables. It takes practice. It also takes courage to put the skills they've learned into action the way Carla did in the story on page 1. Children don't just find that courage in their backpack one day. They learn it from examples set by adults. They learn it through the daily problem-solving and small encounters of school life, such as navigating whom to sit with, how to share space in line, and how to listen to someone even when they disagree.

Why We Need *Responsive School Discipline* More Than Ever

People who have worked in elementary schools for many years share the observation that children are coming to school today with less-well-developed social skills than in past years, regardless of their socioeconomic background. In all grades, children seem to need more instruction in listening, staying on task, cooperating with a partner or small group, being a good loser (or a good winner, for that matter), and being assertive but not aggressive.

At the same time, academic standards have gotten more rigorous. Learning occurs in a social context. So if children are to meet the higher academic demands set before them, schools have to teach the social skills that enable this academic learning, skills like listening with an open mind, self-regulation and self-control, empathy, assertiveness, problem-solving, and taking responsibility. The *Responsive School Discipline* approach gives schools the tools to do this teaching so that children can meet the academic challenges we're setting before them.

Toward Social Skills Learning Standards

Given our children's great need for discipline supports, many educators have come to believe that at the national and state policy levels, we need to place as much emphasis on the teaching of social skills as on the teaching of academic skills. Their belief is bolstered by growing research showing that such social supports work—that they, among other things, correlate with higher academic achievement. (As just one example of such research, a 2001–2004 study by the University of Virginia's Curry School of Education found that in schools using the *Responsive Classroom* approach, children showed greater increases in math and reading test scores, had better social skills, and felt more positive about school [Rimm-Kaufman, 2006].)

So, what if we undertook the same kind of standards-based examination of social learning as we have done with academic learning? What if our mandated state standards included both academic and social skills in a way that recognized the linked nature of the two? What if we thoughtfully integrated key social standards into our curriculum guides, pacing charts, and report cards? Think of the legitimacy and associated supports the teaching of discipline would gain in our schools.

There is movement on this front. As this book goes to press, the U.S. House of Representatives is considering the Academic, Social, and Emotional Learning Act, under which the government would set up a national technical assistance center for social-emotional learning (SEL), provide grants to support evidence-based SEL programming, and conduct a national evaluation of school-based SEL programming ("Latest policy developments," n.d.).

At the state level, in 2004 Illinois became the first state to adopt student social-emotional learning standards, giving those standards equal footing alongside standards in English language arts, math, science, social science, physical development and health, fine arts, and foreign languages (Collaborative for Academic, Social, and Emotional Learning, 2008, p. 2). Now every school district in the state must adopt and submit to the State Board of Education a policy for incorporating social and emotional development into its education program ("Illinois learning standards," 2006). Similar measures have passed or are under consideration in California, New York, Wisconsin, New Jersey, and Ohio ("Latest policy developments," n.d.; "National review of state SEL learning standards," n.d.).

So we have reason to be optimistic. There is action being taken to make social skills teaching the national education concern that it ought to be. At important policy-making levels of the education establishment and in countless schools carrying out the daily work of educating our children, there is a clear and bright vision of social skills learning occupying center stage alongside and integrated with academic learning.

About This Book

The first chapter of this book names a set of key global leadership actions to be taken by school leaders wanting to improve discipline at their school. The rest of the book offers specific strategies for this work. Part 1 focuses on setting the foundations of positive behavior: creating a safe and orderly climate, establishing schoolwide rules, teaching positive behaviors, building school-home partnerships, and ensuring collaborative learning among staff. Part 2 focuses on responding to children's misbehavior: establishing clear response procedures, making sure all staff use them consistently, and, when conferencing with parents is needed, doing so in a respectful, productive way. Finally, Part 3 focuses on discipline on the playground, in the cafeteria, in hallways, and on buses.

Browse, bookmark, dive in, reflect, and discuss with colleagues. You may decide to use some strategies as is and to adapt others to meet your school's needs.

As you lead your school in improving school discipline, keep your eyes on the ultimate goal of optimal student learning. May your work be rigorous, productive, and joyful.

———————————

EDITOR'S NOTE: *As a co-authored work, this book weaves together the voices of two experienced school administrators. The authors share similar convictions and approaches, though they have experienced different schools and educational settings over their careers. This book represents their joint articulation of the essentials of improving school discipline.*

PART ONE

Foundations of Positive Behavior

✦

Seven Key Leadership Actions

Start here to build better discipline

Effective school leadership is crucial to effective school discipline. Look at any school where calm, respectful, and collaborative learning prevails, and you'll find skillful leadership to be a prime factor in the cultivation and maintenance of that climate.

This chapter offers seven key action steps for successfully improving schoolwide discipline:

1. Do a needs assessment.

2. Decide on the scope of your discipline work.

3. Involve all stakeholders.

4. Listen.

5. Develop a shared understanding of your school's discipline approach.

6. Put it in writing.

7. Stop often to reflect.

Whether you're focusing on one specific area of school or launching a comprehensive discipline reform, these leadership actions will help you.

The last action discussed, reflection, may be the most important. Change is an iterative process and requires that school leaders always leave time to take stock of where their school is and where it still needs to go.

Our Most Challenged Children

Sadly, the human face of our children's social skills needs is often that of a child struggling with trauma. In the public school where I served as principal most recently, a significant number of children brought from home the burdens of poverty, drug or alcohol abuse, violence, and incarceration.

Monday mornings at school sometimes felt like Friday nights in an emergency room. Mondays saw a spike in the number of children presenting with trauma from two days of hard family life without the ameliorating supports of school. Too quick to anger, too easily provoked into fights, too close to tears, too preoccupied to follow even simple lessons—this was the norm on Mondays for these children.

B.K. was one such student. A fifth grader, B.K. had trouble getting along with peers because he wasn't keeping up academically, yet he hated to leave the classroom to get extra help because he thought that labeled him a dummy. So he tantrummed to get out of work that was too hard.

Often B.K.'s mom was working when he got out of school, so older siblings or relatives handled his care. B.K. spent more time than he should have with the interventionist, and his mom spent more time than she would have liked in conferences with me.

While his special education teacher worked to create supports that might be effective for him, we expected B.K., like all students, to meet reasonable expectations, ones that were realistic for him and consistent with our school's discipline approach. Did B.K. learn habits of self-regulation fast enough? Will the supports he received carry him through his middle school years and beyond?

Not every child's story will have a completely happy ending, and the jury is still out on B.K. But in another situation, this child's behavior might have landed him in out-of-district placement. I believe it was largely because our school used the *Responsive School Discipline* approach that he remained in regular school and made progress. This approach isn't the only intervention that children such as B.K. need, but it's an important part of their web of support.

1 Do a Needs Assessment

To get a complete picture of where your school is on discipline right now, collect data on discipline referrals to the office, suspensions, and expulsions. Also collect information about the school climate through surveys of parents, teachers, paraprofessionals, bus drivers, and students.

If you see from this data—or if it's simply clear from observation—that your school is an unsafe place, your first task will be to establish order. It will be critical to enforce whatever rules and discipline policies are currently in place with clarity and firm follow-through so that all school members—adults and children—understand your intention to make the school environment safe. The goal is to create enough order for systematic discipline improvement work to go forward.

2 Decide on the Scope of Your Discipline Work

Exactly how best to plan and launch discipline improvement efforts will differ from school to school. Here are two options:

Focus on one area of school

As mentioned in the introduction to this book, you may choose to focus on one specific area of school—recess or lunch, for example. One benefit of this focused approach is that it allows school adults to feel the power of everyone pulling together for one specific goal and to possibly see results sooner. This experience of success will energize them to take on the next challenge.

To choose which area to focus on first, consider which areas of school need attention the most (refer to the data you collected in step 1 above) and balance that against what kind of work your staff and students will likely be successful at now. Make sure the discipline work you embark on is truly needed and a manageable challenge for your school.

Undertake comprehensive reform

An alternative to the focused approach is to reform the school's overall approach to discipline. If you go this route, your main planning and launching tasks will include:

A. Articulating a belief statement about school discipline

B. Creating and celebrating schoolwide rules, a foundational element of positive schoolwide discipline

C. Establishing procedures for handling misbehavior and recommending those procedures to the school council, school committee, or other governing body for approval

Most schools take six to nine months to complete these steps. This means that if you start the process at the beginning of a school year, schoolwide rules could be in place by late winter or spring of the same school year.

It's worthwhile to consider, however, starting the process in January, completing the procedures for handling misbehavior that school year, and opening the following fall with the creation of schoolwide rules, an apt beginning-of-year activity. This would also mean that a belief statement about discipline, a shared understanding of the school's discipline goals and behavior standards, and a policy for handling misbehavior are all in place to support the rule creation activities.

Regardless of the time line you choose, establish a schedule at the outset and clarify who's responsible for what. Many school leaders assemble a leadership team (with representation from the administration, classroom teachers, special area teachers, paraprofessional staff, and parents) to orchestrate the many tasks that will be involved. Think about individuals' available time, interests, leadership skills, and experience when assembling this team, and provide time for the team to meet during the school day.

3 Involve All Stakeholders

Improving school discipline should be a democratic process. This doesn't mean everyone should be at every meeting or be consulted for every step along the way. It does mean, at the very least, keeping everyone informed of the goals, activities, and outcomes of your work and giving everyone a way to voice opinions and concerns.

Consider that your school community has at least these constituents, and possibly more:

■ Students

■ Parents

■ Teachers and other professional staff members

■ Teacher assistants and other paraprofessional staff members

■ Administrators

Even in a small elementary school of 150 children, this list will amount to well over 300 people. In larger schools, the number quickly swells into the thousands. You'll need to install efficient and effective mechanisms to keep two-way communications flowing with all these people (including the children, who will be fascinated to know how the rules will be established, for example, and how they will be a part of the process).

4 Listen

Often school leaders want to fix discipline problems by immediately instituting new discipline policies and practices. But if our discipline work is to produce long-term results, we must take our time with it. If there's an immediate crisis, we can usually find a short-term solution using current practices while we prepare to launch our longer-term work.

Begin this longer-term work by orchestrating conversations about school discipline among all members of the school community—staff, parents, and students. The purpose of these first conversations is not to decide what changes to make, but to help all school members better understand one another's beliefs and expectations around discipline.

Parent questionnaires, principal's open office hours, parent meetings or focus groups, and staff meetings are all opportunities for gathering input from the adults. To gather students' ideas, you can go into classrooms to hold discussions or have teachers hold them and report back at a staff meeting.

At this stage, school leaders' most important job is to listen. Here are important things to listen for from the adults:

- What do parents and staff believe about children's abilities to follow rules, know right from wrong, and learn from their mistakes?

- What do parents want from school staff when it comes to discipline?

- What behaviors do school staff hope parents will reinforce at home?

- What do parents and staff think of the school's current discipline policies and procedures? Which aspects, in their opinion, are working? Which aspects do they think are not working?

Questions to ask students include:

- "What do you think is the most important rule in our school?" (Or "What do you think is the most important rule for the cafeteria [or recess, hallways, and so forth depending on your area of focus]?")

- "What makes you feel safe at school?" (Or "What makes you feel safe at lunch [or recess, in the hallways, and so forth]?")

- "Are there rules you think we should change?"

Seeking such understanding is essential to crafting behavior expectations and policies that are meaningful to and understood by everyone in the school community. Try to suspend, at this early listening stage, any urge to hash out what kind of discipline approach your school should take. For example, if some parents or staff seem to favor a punishment approach to discipline or to believe that discipline is about controlling children, just listen for the time being. Try to understand where they're coming from and acknowledge that everyone's ultimate goal is to see children learning at their best. Later, you'll have time to discuss how the *Responsive School Discipline* approach allows the achievement of that goal in positive ways.

5 Develop a Shared Understanding of Your School's Discipline Approach

Success in implementing your new schoolwide discipline approach depends on everyone in the school community having a solid understanding of it. Make sure everyone knows that the goals of this approach are to ensure that children:

- Feel physically and emotionally safe in school so that they can learn at their best.

- Develop self-discipline and the skills for working and learning cooperatively with others.

Also help everyone understand that all adults must help meet these goals by:

1. Having consistent behavior expectations of students in all school spaces.

2. Teaching students positive behavior throughout the school.

3. Responding to misbehavior in consistent, positive ways.

To ensure that all staff are familiar with your school's discipline approach, discuss it at staff meetings. Look for readings or DVDs to share, and consider sending staff to trainings or conferences that can help them enhance their understanding. (Visit www.responsiveclassroom.org for resources and information.)

If some members of the community seem resistant to or concerned about taking a new or revised discipline approach, it's important to pause and grapple respectfully with the issues. Have honest discussions. Share opinions and questions. Not everyone will agree on everything, but when people feel heard and respected, they'll more often reach agreement and arrive at using common practices.

6 Put It in Writing

Put your school's new discipline approach in writing, and make this writing available to staff and parents. This written documentation should include:

- A belief statement about school discipline. (Or, if you're focusing on discipline in a specific area of your school, a belief statement about discipline in that area.)

■ A description of how your school will teach positive behaviors in classrooms and shared areas such as the playground, cafeteria, hallways, and buses. (Or how your school will teach discipline in just one of these areas if you're taking a focused approach.)

■ The procedures that all staff will consistently use for handling students' misbehavior, including procedures for take-a-break (positive time-out) in a buddy teacher's room or a private, supervised school space; in-school or at-home extended breaks (suspensions); and crisis intervention for extreme misbehaviors. (See Chapters 9–11 for more information.)

Many schools have an official written discipline policy, sometimes called "Rules of Discipline" or "Code of Conduct," that outlines expected behavior, details unacceptable behavior, and spells out consequences for particular offenses in keeping with state and federal law. As part of your discipline improvement work, you'll need to review this document and see whether you need to eventually revise it to make it compatible with both your district's legal requirements and the particular discipline expectations and practices that your school community agrees upon.

7 Stop Often to Reflect

Reflection is the most underused yet most powerful action in bringing about school change. We often skip over it in our hurry, only to end up having to double back, redo steps we glossed over, and pick up fellow travelers we left behind.

We're better served if we slow down to notice and think. Are we including everyone? Is it clear who's responsible for what? Do all school members really have a shared understanding of the school's discipline approach? How deep is our trust of each other? Am I, as a school leader, modeling the respectful ways of interacting with children and colleagues that I'm encouraging in staff?

We're better served if we lift and listen to every voice. Some of the most significant sociological research on school reform has shown that trusting school relationships play a key role in school improvement (Bryk & Schneider, 2002; Bryk et al., 2010). How we work and learn together makes a big difference in what we ultimately achieve in school.

So check for common understanding and a shared sense of direction every step of the way—before a meeting ends, before a vote is taken, before you decide on a set of rules. Reflection helps keep trust among school community members high, long after the rules have become part of the school culture.

CHIP REFLECTS

A Vision of the Possible

What might school discipline reform look like in a school? I can tell you what a key stage of it looked like at Sheffield School, a grade 3–6 school in Turners Falls, Massachusetts, when I was the principal there.

By the fall of 2004, the staff and School Community Council of Sheffield School had spent six months discussing school discipline, arriving at a shared vision, and crafting a written discipline policy. Now we were ready to guide students in creating our schoolwide rules, what we would call the Sheffield Constitution.

We began with each class formulating its own classroom rules. Soon posters with rules like "We will take care of our materials and supplies," "We will be kind to each other," and "We will do our best" could be found in each classroom. Next, delegates from each class took all the rules from their grade and hammered out three or four rules for that grade. Two delegates from each grade then brought these grade-level rules to our "Constitutional Convention" in the superintendent's conference room.

This Constitutional Convention was a big deal. Our school counselor, Kevin White, and I talked about the Constitutional Convention in Philadelphia, how important that had been for our country, and how important this meeting was for our school. Then I gave the students their charge of synthesizing all the grade-level rules into three or four rules for our whole school.

It took awhile for the conversation to get going. After a time I said, "Delegates, you've been working on this for some time now, and you can perhaps have a better discussion without Mr. White and me in the room. We'll wait outside. When you have one rule written on the chart stand here, come out and get us. We'll be right in the hall."

After what felt like an eternity (but what was in reality probably fifteen minutes), a sixth grader asked us to come in. No one in the room spoke. On the chart stand was one word: "ENJOY!"

I cannot tell this story, even today, without getting a little teary, for I knew at that moment that all my beliefs about the goodness of children and their inherent desire for school to be a place of intellectual excitement and enjoyment were being confirmed.

When Kevin and I asked the delegates what they meant by this first rule, they told us, "You know, enjoy your reading, have fun learning math and doing science experiments, feel good about getting better at your work, don't be afraid to make mistakes, stuff like that." These children were expressing their highest hope for school—that it be joyful—and they were wishing that upon all their schoolmates.

After coming up with that first rule, the rest of the list flowed easily. Soon the delegates finalized five schoolwide rules for Sheffield:

> *Enjoy!*
> *Respect everyone and everything around you.*
> *Speak kindly.*
> *Be helpful and responsible.*
> *Take care of classrooms and school property.*

In subsequent years, these rules served Sheffield well. Displayed prominently in the building and kept alive through careful teaching, these rules served as a reminder to the children and adults alike that we wanted our school to be a place of joyful learning and that we would work together to make it so.

(In the years since this rule creation process, Sheffield and two other district schools merged to become a preK–5 school. The new school is revisiting schoolwide rule creation accordingly. For a complete narrative of the first Sheffield School process of developing its schoolwide rules, see Appendix A.)

A Better Definition of "We"

When school leaders say "We're going to improve discipline at our school," who exactly is being identified as the "we"?

In her poem "The Low Road," poet Marge Piercy talks eloquently about the power of people working together to bring about change: *"it starts when you say We / and know who you mean, and each / day you mean one more"* (Piercy, 1980, pp. 44–45).

An important part of building stronger, more positive school discipline is developing a better definition of "we." When all constituents at school are included in this important work, all constituents can pull together. That collaboration is crucial to our children's learning and growth.

Signals for Quiet Attention

SCHOOL LEADER'S CHECKLIST

❑ **Pick one indoor signal**

    ❑ Raised hand (with chime or other auditory component when students are spread out)

    ❑ Other: _____

❑ **Pick one outdoor signal**

    ❑ "Circle up!" or "Allie! Allie!"

    ❑ Whistle

    ❑ Other: _____

❑ **With classroom teachers, introduce students to the signals during the first week of school**

❑ **Teach nonclassroom staff how to use the signals**

    ❑ Playground staff

    ❑ Lunchroom staff

    ❑ Bus supervisors

    ❑ Others: _____

❑ **Use the signals yourself with students and at staff and parent meetings**

Signals for Quiet Attention

Quickly get children's attention anywhere in your school

One of the most effective ways to create a positive school environment is also the simplest: Establish schoolwide signals for quiet attention. Consider the following scenes.

It's lunchtime. Mr. Clark, on lunch duty, wants to give the children a direction. He rings a hand chime and raises his hand. As the calming tone drifts out, the children stop their chatter and give him their attention, most of them raising their hands as well to help spread the visual signal. The other adults in the lunchroom do the same. When everyone is quiet and paying attention, Mr. Clark begins his message to the children.

Out on the playground, Ms. Gilroy wants to gather the children to give them an important safety reminder. She goes to the blacktop and calls out, "Circle up!" The children move in from all directions and form a circle on the blacktop's perimeter. Ms. Gilroy raises her hand, and many of the children copy her. When everyone is quiet and looking at her, Ms. Gilroy begins speaking.

Establishing and consistently using calm, respectful schoolwide signals for quiet attention is a first step in improving school discipline, a step to take even before creating rules. There's a practical reason for this: Signals for attention are relatively easy to teach. By putting them in place first—ideally on the first day of school—we have an immediate way to get children's attention calmly and respectfully. We have the start of effective communication while our other discipline work goes forward.

Such signals send an important message to children. Unlike yelling or shh-ing to get students' attention, which tells children, "We're in a contest. I'll overpower your voice with mine to get your attention," using a raised hand or a pleasant chime says to children, "I respect you. I trust you'll give me your attention if I ask for it using our agreed-upon signal." A calm signal works because of this respect that it conveys.

It also works because a physically raised hand or a chime that can be heard is concrete. As Elena Bodrova and Deborah J. Leong explain in *Tools of the Mind: The Vygotskian Approach to Early Childhood Education*, concrete signals function like graphic symbols or picture cues, helping children better understand what's going on and what's expected of them (Bodrova & Leong, 1995). And it's not just young children who need such concrete tools. The use of quiet signals transforms interactions with upper elementary students as well.

As educators who have used respectful signals in all kinds of schools will attest, such signals, when well devised and well taught, have an almost magical effect. A hand is raised, and silence washes over the room. A chime is rung, and within seconds all motion stops and students turn toward the adult. To bring such effective use of signals to your school, begin with these essentials:

- Establish an indoor and an outdoor signal.

- Expect teachers to teach their students these signals.

- Teach all nonclassroom staff these signals.

- Use these signals yourself.

Establish an Indoor and an Outdoor Signal

At a staff meeting (before the start of the year if you're launching your discipline improvement work at the beginning of a school year), establish with staff an indoor signal for attention that all adults will use in the lunchroom, hallways, and other common spaces. Also establish an outdoor signal for use during recess and field trips.

The most common indoor quiet signal is a raised hand, with an added chime or a handclap pattern for times when children are spread out, such as in the lunchroom, auditorium, or gym. When an adult gives this signal, it means everyone should get quiet and look at the adult. Children may also raise their hands as well to help spread the signal.

Consider your school's style and what students and staff are already comfortable with when you choose a signal. Try to make the schoolwide signal as consistent as possible with any quiet signals children are using in their classrooms.

A common outdoor signal is to call out "Circle up!" or "Allie! Allie!" or to blow a whistle for greater audibility. Students then immediately come from wherever they are, form a circle around the adult, and listen for instructions.

Safety, of course, is one reason for a clear outdoor signal that everyone knows and consistently uses. We need to be able to get children's attention quickly if we want to give them a safety reminder or redirection.

But besides ensuring safety, having a quick way to gather students also simply makes outdoor time more orderly and fun. For example, at the beginning of recess, the adults on duty can give the circle-up signal. The children then gather in a circle and take a moment to pause, breathe, and think before running off to play. At the end of recess, the adults can again give the circle-up signal, and again students gather, taking a few minutes to settle down and shift gears before going back into the building. These brief moments help children make smooth transitions and exercise self-control. (See Chapter 12 for more about recess.)

Expect Teachers to Teach Their Students These Signals

The job of teaching the schoolwide signals falls mostly on classroom teachers (even though school leaders and other staff can reinforce this teaching by practicing the signals in their interactions with students). Expect teachers to do this teaching on the first day of school and to keep practicing it thereafter.

Interactive modeling is a perfect technique for this teaching because it ensures that teachers will show students exactly what the signals look and sound like and exactly how to respond. This specificity is important: If, upon seeing an adult using the raised-hand signal, students are to freeze and look at the adult, teachers need to model what that looks like. If, when an adult calls "Allie! Allie!" the children are to hold on to any equipment they have and bring it with them to the circle, teachers need to show what that looks like. Then students need to be given plenty of chances to practice, and interactive modeling has a built-in step for that practice.

(See Chapter 5 for a description of interactive modeling and recommendations for how to help teachers learn and use the technique.)

CHIP REFLECTS

Have Faith. Wait for Silence.

Quiet signals work only if adults truly wait until all children are giving their attention and are completely quiet—not merely semi-quiet—before speaking. This takes faith. As a principal, my faith was frequently tested. At all-school meetings, facing the unbridled, good-natured chattiness of an auditorium full of children, I often questioned whether waiting with my hand raised would get me anywhere. But I was never disappointed. Gradually the school would begin to quiet, the bubbling turn to a murmur, and the murmur to stillness. Then I would put my hand down and wait another few seconds before speaking, just so we could all hear the quiet.

After a few seconds of complete quiet attention, we would say the Pledge of Allegiance together. After the Pledge, a child would announce, "Please remain standing for a moment of silence."

At the beginning of every school day, the student announcers for the day would also ask for a few seconds of quiet over the intercom before and after leading the school in saying the Pledge.

In these moments of silence, the whole school felt as one.

Teach All Nonclassroom Staff These Signals

At a meeting before school starts in the fall, teach all nonclassroom staff—lunchroom and recess supervisors, custodians, bus supervisors, and so forth—your schoolwide signals for attention. It's crucial that all these adults use these signals the way the children will be taught by their classroom teachers. This consistency is essential to an orderly, calm climate in all common spaces in the school.

Use the Signals Yourself

No one's example is more important than the school leader's. When you lead all-school meetings, drop in on lunch, or take your turn supervising recess, be sure to use your school's signals for attention exactly as all the adults agreed to use them and as taught to students. Your example will help turn the use of these signals into a schoolwide habit. And it will send the message to adults and children alike that the school is serious about always using a respectful way to get children's attention.

USING SIGNALS EFFECTIVELY

- **Don't negotiate with students.** Whether to have a signal, what it should be, and how to respond to it should never be negotiated with students. Have teachers simply explain why a signal is needed and teach it on or near the first day of school.

- **Insist on consistency among staff.** This consistency shows students that all the adults are serious about the signals, which can be reassuring to children. If you notice adults differing in how they use schoolwide signals, bring up the issue at a meeting. Find out if the reason for the inconsistency is that the signals need adjusting.

- **Insist on quiet after a signal.** After giving a signal, it can be tempting to start speaking before all students are quiet, especially if they're slow to get quiet. Let staff know that in these situations, they should instead give the signal again and wait (while making a mental note to reteach the signal at their next opportunity). This reinforces that the adults are serious when they expect students to respect the signal.

■ **Give children a few seconds.** It's important to insist that children get quiet after a signal, but immediate silence is not necessary. It's more respectful and realistic to give children several seconds to get to a natural stopping point in their conversation or task. It's also not necessary to require all students to raise their hands when they see an adult raise hers. The point is for enough students to do so to help spread the signal.

F I N A L   T H O U G H T

Hold Adults to the Same Expectations

Make sure all adults in your school show respect for schoolwide signals as well. We're all familiar with this scene: A lunch supervisor raises her hand and rings a chime for quiet attention. Students throughout the lunchroom quiet down and many raise their hands as well to help spread the signal. Meanwhile two other adults in the room dutifully raise their hands but continue to whisper to each other while the lunch supervisor speaks to the children. Soon a few children start to talk to each other as well, then a few more.

When adults continue to talk over the signal, students are likely to do the same. Impress this upon all staff, and also explain the signal to school visitors. Being firm with the adults as well as the children helps preserve the power of quiet signals.

Schoolwide Rules

SCHOOL LEADER'S CHECKLIST

❑ **Generate schoolwide rules**

    ❑ Decide: Revise existing school rules or develop fresh rules from scratch?

    ❑ Decide: Involve adults only or also include the children?

❑ **Articulate expectations for specific areas of school (playground, cafeteria, hallways, buses)**

    ❑ Decide: Apply schoolwide rules to these areas or create area-specific rules?

    ❑ Lead relevant staff in naming what each school area would look like if the rules were being followed

❑ **Celebrate the rules with an "unveiling" or other all-school activity**

❑ **Teach the rules**

    ❑ Get staff input on which behaviors need the most attention

    ❑ Arrange for lunch, recess, and bus supervisors to be present at the teaching if possible

    ❑ Provide professional development in positive adult language and interactive modeling

    ❑ Lead the teaching effort yourself

Schoolwide Rules

Create a few positive rules that apply everywhere in school

Keep our school clean and green.
Act in ways that make our school safe, caring, and welcoming.
Do your best learning.
Help others do their best learning.

These simple statements typify the kind of schoolwide rules that are crucial to effective discipline. Positively stated and easy for children to understand, such schoolwide rules provide students with a daily reminder of the behaviors expected of them. They also communicate to the entire school community—children, teachers, other school adults, and parents—the ideals for rigorous and joyful learning that guide life at the school.

Although many teachers engage students in creating rules for their own classrooms, having a set of overarching schoolwide rules sends children the important message that we expect all school members to meet the same high standards of behavior everywhere at school, not just in their classrooms.

Having schoolwide rules also gives all staff a concrete basis for guiding children toward positive behavior. When teachers teach students how to conduct themselves outside the classroom, they can say "One of our school-wide rules is to keep our school clean and green. How might we put that rule into action in the lunchroom?" This then leads perfectly into a discussion and interactive modeling of lunchroom routines.

When lunch and recess supervisors and other nonclassroom staff see inappropriate behavior, they can refer to the rules when they respond. For example, a recess supervisor can say "Greta, remember our school rule 'Be kind'? Try the swings again with that rule in mind."

How you lead your school to come up with or revise schoolwide rules will depend on your school's specific needs and character. Some schools engage students in the process; others involve only adults. The exact content and format of the rules also differs from school to school.

Regardless of these variations, however, schoolwide rules should always communicate a school's values and aspirations. The rules should help answer the question "What do we want our school culture to be, and what are our individual and collective responsibilities for creating and maintaining this culture?"

Here are examples of schoolwide rules that fit this description from two other schools:

Treat others the way you would want to be treated.
Keep everyone safe and healthy.
Take care of our school and classroom materials.
Be a respectful learner.

Be safe.
Be respectful.
Take care of school property.
Do your best work.

Once your school establishes its rules, expect teachers to teach and talk about them with students. Celebrate the rules. Expect adults to refer to the rules when guiding student behavior day in and day out. Model this frequent referencing of the rules yourself. Only through this active use will schoolwide rules continue to have meaning for students.

To establish and keep alive meaningful schoolwide rules, lead your school through these steps:

- Envision what school should look and feel like.
- Generate the schoolwide rules.
- Articulate expectations for specific areas of school.
- Celebrate the rules.
- Teach the rules.

Envision What School Should Look and Feel Like

Since the purpose of schoolwide rules is ultimately to create an environment that allows for optimal student learning, begin the rule creation process by asking school stakeholders "What would our school look, sound, and feel like if all students were doing their best learning?"

Use your school's mission statement as a springboard

One way to lead this discussion is to bring out your school's mission or vision statement at a meeting of school community adults. Ask everyone to consider afresh the statement's words and phrases. Ask what they would see and hear around school if this mission or vision were realized.

For example, the Future Leaders Institute (FLI) Charter School in New York City had a statement reading, in part, "to create a respectful and open environment equally conducive to diligence and imagination." What would a "respectful and open environment" look like throughout the building? How would teachers and students be behaving and interacting throughout the day? What would an observer see in such an environment? Similarly, what would "diligent and imaginative" children be doing? Would they be happily engaged in conversations or projects? Would they be independently managing materials and supplies and sharing resources and ideas?

Ask open-ended questions

Alternatively, you can lead a discussion by asking the following questions:

- Think of a time when children were most engaged with their learning. What was happening? How were individuals behaving and inter-acting with one another?

- Think about morning arrival time, the middle of the day, and after-noon dismissal time. How, ideally, would students be behaving and interacting?

- What would adults be doing if they were supporting children in these behaviors and interactions? What would teachers be doing? What would the lunch, recess, and other staff be doing? What would school leaders be doing?

Bring in parents' goals

Remember to bring parents' aspirations and hopes into this envisioning process. Here are two ways:

- **Survey parents.** Send (or have teachers send) a survey to parents before the school year starts. Ask them about their goals for their child that year.

- **Instruct teachers to talk with parents.** Make sure teachers invite parents to talk about their goals for their children during the first parent-teacher conference of the year.

These parent goals then become part of school adults' consciousness and inform the whole envisioning process.

Generate the Schoolwide Rules

After articulating what your school would ideally look and feel like, it's time to generate a set of schoolwide rules that would enable that ideal to be achieved. There are several ways to do this. You can lead your school to revise existing school rules or to develop fresh rules from scratch. You can involve only adults or also meaningfully engage students in this process (see Appendix A for one sample process that involves the whole school).

Regardless of what process you choose, the rules you end up with should be positively, broadly, and inspiringly stated; developmentally appropriate; and few in number. (See "Rules That Work" on page 37 for more about effective rules.)

One way to arrive at rules that fit this description is to gather staff together and lead them through the following steps:

- **Brainstorm succinct rules.** Ask staff for rules that answer the question "What positive behaviors throughout the school would help turn our envisioned ideal school into reality?" Although it's important to end up with only a few final rules, there's value in putting all ideas on the table at this stage. Doing so can surface differences of opinion that can spark great discussions and ultimately lead to stronger consensus and investment.

  Help staff make their wording succinct. For example, if someone suggests "Use quiet voices and walking feet when moving through the school building so that others can do their best learning and no one gets hurt," help the individual turn that into the more concise "Use quiet voices and walking feet" or "Move safely and act responsibly."

- **Sort the brainstormed list into three to five categories.** Typically, brainstormed ideas can be sorted into these broad areas:

  - Responsibility for self (rules about students keeping themselves safe and learning at their best)

  - Responsibility toward others (rules about being considerate of others and allowing them to learn at their best)

  - Responsibility for the environment (rules about maintaining the physical space, materials, and tools)

  Of course, many rules will fit into multiple categories. Let staff know that the point is to create reasonable categories, not to find the absolute "correct" category for each rule.

- **Consolidate each category.** In this final step, lead staff in consolidating the ideas in each category into one concise statement that encompasses all the individual ideas. These few global statements then become the final schoolwide rules.

Here's an example:

Brainstormed Ideas, Categorized	Consolidated Final Rules
Responsibility for self: Follow the dress code. Use appropriate voice level and language. Follow directions. Work and play safely. Make responsible choices. Give your personal best. Accept responsibility. Listen and learn. Model safe behavior. Be open to new ideas. Be creative and inquisitive. Ask questions. Follow schoolwide signal for quiet.	*Always do your best to be safe, responsible, and open to learning.*
Responsibility toward others: Keep hands, feet, objects, and hurtful comments to yourself. Earn and give respect. Work as a team. Listen when others are speaking.	*Earn and give respect through your words and actions.*
Responsibility for environment: Keep school graffiti-free. Take care of materials and space. Keep school clean. Reduce, reuse, and recycle. Respect others' space and property.	*Help keep our school safe, clean, and green.*

RULES THAT WORK

School rules are most effective when they're:

■ **Stated in positive terms.** Rules are more effective if they tell children what to do rather than what not to do. For example, instead of "No fighting," try "Solve problems peacefully." Although both statements address the safety and well-being of school members, "No fighting" sells children short by assuming that many of them are prone to fighting. It also doesn't communicate what we expect to see, if not fighting. By contrast, "Solve problems peacefully" conveys the belief that children are capable of solving problems peacefully. And rather than issuing restrictions, it inspires children to imagine peaceful actions.

■ **Worded broadly and inspiringly.** The best rules are broad enough to encompass many specific behaviors and inspiring enough to feel important to children. "Walk throughout the building," for example, narrowly dictates one behavior and doesn't invite children to think. "Show respect for our learning environment," however, engages children's imagination ("What does respect look like in different situations?" "What makes an environment good for learning?" "What does 'environment' mean here?").

■ **Developmentally appropriate.** For example, some schools have a "zero voices" rule for common spaces in the building. But is it reasonable to expect elementary students to be totally silent when moving through the halls or while eating lunch? For that matter, are adults using zero voices in the common spaces? Instead of "Zero voices," a more effective rule might be "Quiet voices," which has the same intention of ensuring a low noise level while being more developmentally appropriate.

■ **Few in number and brief in wording.** While there's no magical right number, most schools find that it's effective to have three to five schoolwide rules. Each rule should also be short. Children tend to tune out when presented with a long list of wordy rules.

Good Rules Inspire Big Thinking

The best school rules not only guide school behavior, but also stimulate broad thinking about how to learn and live peacefully in the larger community as well. I was reminded of this while reading *The Kindness Handbook* by Sharon Salzberg.

In her book, Salzberg talks about leading a workshop at a Washington, DC, elementary school. She noticed school rules posted throughout the school's hallways, simple rules that had great potential to inspire children and adults toward kindness: "Everyone can play; Help others when they need help; Treat people the way you would like to be treated; Respect everyone—other students and all staff."

Salzberg began to imagine how powerful these rules would be if people truly lived by them in their daily lives. She was so inspired that she decided to take one of the rules each week and hold it as a personal touchstone, paying great attention to that rule in all her choices and interactions with others. One of the rules, "Everyone can play," was particularly meaningful to Salzberg. She found herself including others more in conversation and, as a result, noticed a greater sense of "rightness and balance" in her life.

Thoughtfully created school rules do this. They inspire everyone they touch toward kindness, respect, responsibility, peacefulness, and collaboration. Our students may not be able to articulate how they've been transformed by good school rules the way Salzberg did. But realized and articulated or not, the transformation will be there if we create rules carefully and then follow up with daily positive teaching and support.

Articulate Expectations for Specific Areas of School

If your schoolwide rules are well conceived and well worded, they should be relevant in all school spaces, including the playground, cafeteria, hallways, and buses. It's still important, however, to lead your staff in articulating specific expectations for these areas.

This deliberate articulation ensures that everyone has the same picture of acceptable and unacceptable behaviors in these parts of school. It also sends a message from the school leadership that these times and areas of school are integral parts of the learning day, as important as the math or language arts period.

Options for articulating expectations for specific areas of school:

Discuss how schoolwide rules apply

Lead staff (and devise a way to involve students if appropriate) in naming what each area of school would look and sound like if the schoolwide rules were being followed. Ask open-ended questions such as:

- "What are our goals for this time of day?"

- For adults: "What do we hope children will experience or learn during recess (or at lunch, in the halls, or on the bus)? What student behaviors will enable this? What adult behavior will reinforce such behaviors?"

- For children: "What would make recess (or lunch, the halls, or the bus ride) nice? What would people be doing? How would you be feeling?"

Consider holding grade-level teacher conversations first so that teachers can agree on expectations for their grade and then bringing all teachers together to identify common elements across all grades.

Create area-specific rules

If playground, lunchroom, hallway, or bus behavior is a problem at your school, it would be beneficial to create specific rules for these places. Use the schoolwide rule creation process described previously to generate these area-specific rules as well. (See Chapters 12–15 for more on area-specific rules.)

Celebrate the Rules

Once you have a set of schoolwide rules, celebrate them! Come up with a way to "unveil" them to the school community that signals their importance. This could be as simple as the principal and assistant principal visiting each classroom to share the schoolwide rules with students during morning meetings.

Or the celebration can be more elaborate. At Mt. Pleasant Elementary in Wilmington, Delaware, the assistant principal, a former music teacher, enlisted students to help create a rap song about the rules, which was performed at an all-school assembly and periodically thereafter during morning all-school announcements. At Sheffield School in Turners Falls, Massachusetts, the entire school held a rules ratification ceremony at which students, staff, and parents affirmed their schoolwide rules with a voice vote and a standing ovation.

Even when rules are firmly established and remain the same from year to year, find a way to celebrate them each year to keep them alive. Beauvoir, the National Cathedral Elementary School in Washington, DC, posted its schoolwide rules near the entrance after they were created. One year, as part of a larger effort to reinforce students' interest and skill in math, the school invited students, staff, and visitors to put a sticker next to their favorite rule. The stickers resulted in a giant bar graph on the wall. This called fresh attention to the schoolwide rules and prompted the entire school community to reflect on the meaning of each specific rule.

Teach the Rules

Rules have meaning only if we actively teach them to children. When it comes to schoolwide rules, this means teaching students how to translate the rules into action in various school situations and helping students see the rules as meaningful guides for their behavior. Here are important leadership steps you can take to ensure that this happens at your school:

- **Develop a plan for how every child in school will be taught.** Classroom teachers will be the ones doing most of the teaching of schoolwide rules. Plan how this will be accomplished. For example, when will teachers take their classes to the lunchroom for lessons on what following the rules might look and sound like there? How about the playground? The auditorium? What schedules do you need to create?

Can you arrange for lunch and recess paraprofessionals, bus supervisors, and bus drivers to be present during at least some of these lessons? Their presence will help ensure that all adults are on the same page regarding what behaviors are expected.

■ **Get staff input on which behaviors need to be taught the most.** Lead a staff conversation on which behaviors are hardest for or most confusing to students in the common spaces. Include lunch and recess paraprofessionals and, if possible, any bus supervisors in this conversation. Find a way to get bus drivers' input as well. These adults' ideas are invaluable, since they spend the most time with students in these spaces. Then have teachers focus on these behaviors when they teach students the schoolwide rules.

■ **Provide professional development in positive adult language and interactive modeling.** Many teachers use these two *Responsive Classroom* practices to teach students expected behaviors in their classrooms. They are key practices for the teaching of rules outside the classroom as well—so important that this book devotes a chapter to each (see Chapter 4 for positive adult language and Chapter 5 for interactive modeling). Reserve time at staff meetings to introduce these techniques to staff and allow staff to practice with each other. And model using these techniques yourself in your interactions with students.

■ **Lead the teaching effort.** Although the teaching of schoolwide rules rests mainly with classroom teachers, it's so important for school leaders to lead the effort. Signal to staff that you expect them to take time at the beginning of the year to intensively teach the rules. To set an example, take some classes to the playground or lunchroom and do this teaching yourself. Draw attention to the rules during all-school gatherings. Devote staff meeting time to teacher discussion and practice of how best to teach and reinforce rules. Finally, spend time reflecting with staff on which rules are working well and which might need continued focus and attention.

■ **Publicly reinforce the rules all year long.** After the intensive teaching in the first weeks of school, keep the rules alive throughout the year with quick, positive references to them throughout the day, every day. It makes a big difference when students hear you saying things such as "I saw lots of you following our schoolwide rule 'Make our school safe, caring, and welcoming' at today's assembly. I heard kind words and saw friendly expressions" and "Before we go to recess, who can remind everyone what our rule 'Keep everyone safe and healthy' might look like on the playground?"

BABS REFLECTS

Rules Apply to Adults, Too

Children are keen observers. They learn more from what we adults do than what we say. If "Respect the learning environment" is one of our schoolwide rules but school leaders broadcast frequent messages on the PA system that interrupt student learning, then we're telling the children that we don't really stand behind that rule. If we expect children to earn and give respect, then we must also strive to earn and give respect—in our interactions with colleagues and students.

When teachers or administrators fail to abide by a rule, the rule loses its potency. The school takes on a "do as I say, not as I do" culture. It's easy to understand why students may then do what's expected when an adult is watching but revert to "anything goes" when out of sight of adults.

We'd be wise, then, to examine our own behaviors, not just children's, when we think about rules. What does being safe, responsible, and open to learning mean for us, the adults in the building? How will we give and earn respect through our words and actions toward children? What about toward colleagues? What will safety, responsibility, and openness look like when we encounter each other in the office, and on the playground, and in the lunchroom? How will we contribute to a more positive learning community?

FINAL THOUGHT

Keep Checking: Do Our Rules Need Adjustment?

Rules should stay relevant to our school community over time. This means frequently asking *Are our schoolwide rules contributing to a safe and joyful learning environment? Are they providing enough information to the children? Are we teaching the rules continuously, not just during the first few weeks of school?* It's important for school leaders to facilitate this reflection at all levels—with teachers, students, other school leaders, and parents.

Stopping to check like this provides valuable information. You may find that some children are feeling unsafe during some part of their day. Or you may see that the wording of the rules needs to be adjusted, or the teaching of social competencies ramped up. Schools are living organizations in constant flux. Ongoing assessments allow the rules to keep pace and our schools to remain strong learning communities.

Positive Adult Language

SCHOOL LEADER'S CHECKLIST

❑ **Devote staff meeting time to positive language**

❑ **Provide training for paraprofessionals**

❑ **Emphasize these essentials of positive language to all staff:**

  ❑ Convey belief in children

  ❑ Be direct

  ❑ Use reinforcing language when children show positive behaviors

  ❑ Use reminding language before or just when children start to forget expectations

  ❑ Use redirecting language when children's behavior has gone off track

❑ **Use positive language yourself**

❑ **Organize staff visits to classrooms**

❑ **Recognize staff progress**

CHAPTER 4

Positive Adult Language

Support children's learning with this powerful tool

"Hello, Tasha! How's your new baby brother?" the principal says as she greets a student in the hallway during morning arrival. Just then a teacher comments to a student at his classroom door, "Good morning, Aliya. It's so nice to see you. I notice you remembered to walk quietly and safely in the hall the way we practiced." A moment later, the school counselor firmly and respectfully says to a student, "Nolan, remember, friendly words," when Nolan starts to speak harshly to another student in the hall.

■ ■ ■

Walk into any school, spend five minutes listening to how the adults talk, and you'll get a sense of what they believe about children and how they teach discipline. In the scene above, it's easy to see—and hear—that the adults at this school care about and know the students, believe in them, and see discipline as being about enabling children to choose positive behaviors. It's clear that this school is a welcoming place. This positive approach to discipline and the overall tone of safety and caring is largely set by the adults' language—what they say and how they say it.

Positive adult language, or the professional use of words and tone of voice to enable students to learn in an engaged, active way and to develop positive behaviors, is a critical tool in building school discipline. It's so important because our choice of words, our intentions behind those words, and the

45

manner in which we deliver our words all have a profound effect on how students perceive themselves and their world. Through our language, we can encourage children to see themselves as capable, responsible students and rule respecters and to feel that their school is a place of important learning. This view of themselves and their school is essential if children are to choose and maintain positive behaviors.

Given the importance of language, it's critical that all adults in the school use positive language so that it becomes the school norm. Many of the classroom teachers in your school may already use positive language to ensure discipline in their classrooms and to teach students expected behaviors in the school's common spaces. But it's important that recess, lunch, and bus supervisors and all other staff use positive language as well so that children experience this kind of discipline support everywhere they go, from every adult they interact with. Children need this consistency if they're to achieve and maintain expected behaviors schoolwide.

This chapter offers strategies for helping all your school's staff learn and use positive language and then outlines the important points about positive language to convey to staff as you do this work. (For more details about positive language, see *The Power of Our Words: Teacher Language That Helps Children Learn* by Paula Denton, 2007, available from www.responsiveclassroom.org.)

How to Ensure All Staff Learn and Use Positive Language

Here are effective strategies for achieving positive adult language schoolwide:

- Devote staff meeting time to talking about positive language.

- Provide training for paraprofessionals.

- Form study groups on positive language.

- Use positive language yourself with students and adults.

- Organize staff visits to classrooms.

- Recognize staff progress in using positive language.

Devote staff meeting time to talking about positive language

To ensure that all teachers learn and use positive language with students, regularly talk about this strategy at staff meetings (see "Essentials of Positive Language to Emphasize to All Staff" on page 49). Take time to address specific aspects of positive language, make the discussions interactive, and give teachers time to practice the skills you're focusing on. For example, in a discussion of reinforcing language, you might lead a brief exercise in which teachers name positive student behaviors they saw recently. Ask the group, "How did you or could you reinforce these behaviors using specific and descriptive language?" Have teachers try out some wordings in small groups and then report back to the whole group.

Grade-level meetings are another great opportunity for teachers to build their language skills. Expect the leaders of these meetings to regularly spend time on this topic. For example, the leaders might have the assembled colleagues identify important skills that children will need for success at various times of the day. Colleagues could then work together in partnerships or small groups to plan and practice the reinforcing, reminding, and redirecting language they might use when teaching these skills.

Provide training for paraprofessionals

Be sure to provide training in positive language for other school adults as well, especially the recess, lunch, and bus paraprofessionals, so that they'll speak in supportive ways as they interact with students. Plan when these trainings will take place and who will lead them—whether you or a teacher who's skillful in using positive language.

If your school has chosen to focus its discipline work on one specific area of school—the lunchroom or the playground, for instance—prioritize training for the staff who work in that area. Use real behavior situations they often face when guiding them in practicing effective language for handling misbehavior. (For an example of such training for cafeteria paraprofessionals, see page 198 in Chapter 13.)

Form study groups on positive language

To supplement the staff trainings on positive language, organize (or encourage teacher leaders to organize) study groups for teachers and other staff to delve more deeply into the strategy. Groups can read books and articles or watch videos on positive language and then reflect on them together. You can be very influential in raising interest and investment in study groups by leading or joining them yourself.

Two useful resources for study groups on language are the book *The Power of Our Words: Teacher Language That Helps Children Learn* by Paula Denton and the *Teacher Language Professional Development Kit*, which includes video clips, a facilitator's guide, and session booklets. (Both resources are available from www.responsiveclassroom.org.)

Use positive language yourself with students and adults

We school leaders need to "walk the talk." Pay attention to how you use language with staff and students. When you talk to or about students, be sure you convey belief in the children's positive intentions and abilities. Be sure to convey belief in staff's positive intentions and abilities as well. When you talk to or about families, check that your language includes and honors all students' family cultures.

One natural and particularly important time for school leaders to model positive language for the school is recess and lunch. Regularly go to at least part of recess and lunch. Staff can learn a lot from hearing how you use language to help children meet expectations during this often challenging time of the day.

Organize staff visits to classrooms

If certain teachers are strong in their use of positive language, establish a system in which other classroom teachers, specialists, and nonteaching staff visit their rooms. Hearing colleagues in action can be an effective way for staff to develop their own language skills. For maximum benefit, institute short debriefings after these visits, in which the visiting and visited adults reflect together about how they can use positive language more consistently.

For instance, a classroom teacher and a PE teacher might together come up with language to facilitate a calm, orderly transition to PE. A lunchroom aide and a classroom teacher could agree on ways to remind children to welcome others to their lunch table. The more such conversation there is between colleagues, the more positive students' behavior is likely to be throughout the school.

Recognize staff progress in using positive language

After trainings, study groups, and visits focused on positive language, listen for changes in the way staff talk to children. Then comment about it. Letting staff know you noticed powerfully raises their awareness of this discipline strategy and signals that you see it as an expected practice at your school.

Essentials of Positive Language to Emphasize to All Staff

In trainings and conversations about positive language, emphasize that adults should do the following when speaking to students:

- Convey belief in children.

- Be direct.

- Use reinforcing language when children show positive behaviors.

- Use reminding language before or just when children start to forget expectations.

- Use redirecting language when children's behavior has gone off track.

- Show friendly interest in children's home lives.

- Don't overcorrect children's English.

Convey belief in children

Ask staff to imagine what it would be like to attend a school where every adult assumed the best of them and communicated a belief in their ability to be a successful student. Encourage staff to let their own conviction about children's desire and ability to do well come through when they speak to students.

For example, compare these two ways of talking to a student at the start of the day:

1. *"Shayna, don't you even think about running to your classroom this morning. I'm watching you!"*

2. *"Good morning, Shayna, I'm so glad you're here today. I see you're remembering to walk safely in the hall."*

Point out that these two ways of talking send very different messages:

- The first way communicates a lack of faith in Shayna's ability to follow the rules. It also sets up the adult as an "enforcer," undermining trust between the adult and student.

- The second way communicates that the adult sees Shayna's good intentions and responsible behavior and, most importantly, believes that she can succeed.

Help staff see that the second way of talking helps Shayna internalize a positive identity and develop more self-awareness and self-control. It also helps others within earshot form a positive perception of Shayna, which further enhances the child's self-perception and behavior.

Be direct

Whether giving directions, noting positive behaviors, prompting children to remember rules, stopping misbehavior, or holding a discussion, it's important that adults' language is direct and authentic, free of innuendo or sarcasm.

Here's an example to share with staff: It's lunchtime, and a class of fifth graders is making their way to the cafeteria, with their teacher walking alongside the line. Suddenly a student further back in line jumps up and smacks the doorframe with his hand. The teacher quietly walks to the student and says in a neutral, matter-of-fact voice, "Go back to the end of the hall and try that again, following our hallway rules." The student drops out of line and re-navigates the hallway, this time safely and considerately. The teacher responds with a friendly smile and gestures for him to join the class in line.

Point out that in this example, the teacher communicated clearly and directly. His choice of words, tone of voice, facial expression, and body posture all communicated calmness and respect. In this way, he kept the focus on the child's misbehavior without judging or shaming the child and quickly re-established order. Had he lectured or used sarcasm or innuendo, a power struggle might have ensued and the outcome might have been completely different.

You may want to show staff the table on the opposite page.

Direct Language

Instead of:	Try:
Manipulating children's behavior by holding up classmates as exemplars "Look how nicely Bobby and Clarence are standing in line" (announced to the class to get a few children to stop pushing in the line).	**Telling the children directly what to do** "Maria, Paul, and George, join me at the end of the line. Show me how to follow our hands-off rule" (said quietly to the three students).
Phrasing directions as questions "Could you please wait your turn to speak?"	**Phrasing directions as directions** "It's time to listen" (in a matter-of-fact tone with a raised-hand signal for attention).
Using sarcasm "Samantha, you're in fourth grade. Our first graders follow rules better than you. Why am I not surprised by your behavior?"	**Pointing child in the positive direction** "Samantha, stop. Walk to your classroom. I'll watch you from here" (in a firm tone).
Generalizing about a child's motivation "You're trying to test my patience, aren't you? I think you enjoy starting arguments during recess."	**Figuring out what's going on for a child** "It looks like recess is a hard time of day for you. What's happening at recess that makes it hard to remember our safety rules?"
Pulling in negative history "Taylor, we've talked about this many times. How many times do I have to remind you to keep your hands to yourself when walking in line?"	**Remaining in the present moment** "Taylor, hands to yourself in the hall. Come walk with me."

Use reinforcing language when children show positive behaviors

Reinforcing language identifies and affirms students' specific positive actions. This kind of language encourages children to continue their appropriate behavior. To a group who showed welcoming behavior toward each other at lunch, an adult might say, "I noticed so many people including everyone at their lunch table in conversation. There was a lot of discussion about yesterday's snow day. I heard many open-ended questions that helped people feel a part of the conversation."

Point out to staff that when we take the time to name what children are specifically doing well, we're letting children know that we see them for their positive contributions. This is important for all students, but particularly important for discouraged or troubled students, who may be accustomed to being "seen" by adults only when they fall short of expectations.

In appropriate situations, we can add a question to further extend children's thinking. "Natalie, this week you had only one take-a-break during recess games. This is a big improvement from last week. What helped you to stay calm during our games?" Such a question strengthens children's ability to name, for themselves, constructive behaviors and helps them develop self-discipline.

REINFORCING LANGUAGE: TO-DO'S TO HIGHLIGHT FOR STAFF

- **Name concrete, specific behaviors.** An art teacher says to a class, "Students, your hopes and dreams display shows that you put careful thought into what you want to learn in art this year. Your illustrations show so much detail." Unlike "Good job!" or "Beautiful work!" or other such phrases of global praise, the naming of specific behaviors lets children know what exactly they're doing successfully and therefore what exactly to keep doing and build on.

- **Use a warm and professional tone.** A cafeteria aide tells a student, "Tanya, you remembered our five-finger rule. You selected a meat, two vegetables, a drink, and dessert. That's a healthy and complete lunch."

■ **Emphasize description over personal approval.** A bus driver remarks to a bus group, "You were friendly and safe on the bus today. When you stay in your seats and talk to your seatmates, the ride is more pleasant for everyone." This is more powerful than "You were friendly and safe on the bus today. I like it when you stay in your seats and talk to your seatmates" because it focuses on the group's well-being rather than the adult's personal feelings.

■ **Find positives to name in all students.** This includes students who tend to have trouble with behavior. An assistant principal says to a child who was in the office the day before for misbehavior, "Clayton, your teacher says you've had a great morning. She said you finished all your work and you might be reading a story to your kindergarten buddy this afternoon. You're staying focused during writing time. What strategies are helping you do that?"

■ **Name progress, even if a goal hasn't been fully reached.** A student at an all-school meeting interrupts a classmate and then catches himself mid-sentence. Later, his teacher says to him privately, "Billy, you caught yourself and stopped talking when Jackson was sharing. You're getting better at holding on to your good ideas until it's your turn to talk." It's important, however, to name only those behaviors that students truly demonstrated, rather than ones we're still hoping for. Saying "I see children working hard" when the group is chatting off-task can feel manipulative to the children.

Use reminding language before or just when children start to forget expectations

Reminding language prompts children to recall expectations. Before children go into an activity that might be a bit challenging, adults can set them up for success by giving them a reminder. "Before we line up for PE," a teacher might say to a class, "remember how we practiced being safe and kind in the hallway. Take a moment to think about that."

We can also use reminding language to pull children back just as they're beginning to act inappropriately. A recess teacher sees Zoe holding on to the ball for longer than her turn and immediately says, "Zoe, recess rules." Zoe passes the ball to someone else, and a dispute over equipment is averted.

■ **Name expectations clearly.** An instructional aide reminds a student, "Garrett, hallway rules say that we need to move safely. Show me what that will look like."

■ **Use a direct tone and neutral body language.** Some students are having a hard time settling down for an all-school meeting. "What should you be doing right now?" their teacher asks them in a neutral, sarcasm-free manner.

■ **Anticipate potential behavior problems.** Knowing that the upcoming fire drill can be a challenge for the class, a teacher says to them, "What do you need to do when you hear the fire alarm today during our fire drill?"

■ **Issue reminders early.** Right when children are beginning to play roughly on the slide, rather than later when their roughness escalates and is harder to reverse, a recess supervisor says, "Play safely and kindly. Show me now."

■ **Keep it brief.** A group at a cafeteria cleanup station is throwing recyclables into the trash. A custodian, aware that students tend to tune out long strings of words, says simply, "Remember our recycling rules."

Use redirecting language when children's behavior has gone off track

Redirecting language commands children to do something different than what they're currently doing. In the course of any school day, there are many times when children's behavior needs to be interrupted immediately and swiftly to maintain safety or to protect the positive learning tone. And there are times when children have gone too far down the path of misbehaving to be pulled back with a reminder. These are the times to use redirecting language.

Emphasize to school adults that when redirecting children, they need to calmly tell the children exactly what to do. "Leah, stop," "James, freeze. Take a break," or "Trudy, carry the chair with the legs pointing down."

A Lesson From the River

While paddling the rapids of the Salmon River in Idaho with my husband on a vacation some years ago, I learned an important lesson that carried over to my work in schools. Tom and I were in our raft, fast approaching a large boulder in the river's bend, a spot we had been warned to avoid during our briefing earlier by Paul, our guide. The trouble was we couldn't remember what Paul had said we should do to navigate this particular rapid.

Our fellow travelers were shouting from their nearby rafts, "Don't hit the rock! Don't hit the rock!" Well, it was clear we didn't want to hit the rock, but we needed some guidance on how—which moves to make to avoid the churning water that was rapidly sucking our boat right into the rock. Before I knew it, we hit the boulder and Tom flipped out of the boat. Luckily he was unhurt and managed to hang on to the raft while Paul rescued us.

Throughout the rest of the day, Tom and I practiced our back paddling and ferrying skills as we made our way on down the river. When Paul said "back paddle," we back paddled. When Paul said "pull right," we pulled right. Paul's clear and action-oriented directions kept us safe for the rest of the trip.

This made me think of all of the times we adults "warn" children against dangerous behavior ("Don't push on the playground," "Don't slide tackle during recess soccer," "Don't put your hands on others"). These types of warnings, instead of pointing children in positive directions, just bring attention to negative behaviors. And as I learned on the Salmon River, when their raft is out of control, we shouldn't tell children what not to do. We need to tell them—clearly, briefly, and directly—what *to* do. My river experience was a huge reminder of the importance of emphasizing this point when helping teachers and other school staff learn to use effective language with students.

- **Name desired, not undesired, behavior.** A PE teacher says to a student, "Freeze. Come stand by me for a minute. Now try the water fountain line again, keeping your hands to yourself" instead of "Don't push in line at the water fountain!"

- **Phrase redirections as commands, not questions.** "Manny, come here," a recess supervisor says. "Tag gently. OK, try again. I'll watch you" instead of "Manny, come here. Listen, can you tag gently?"

- **Say only what you want the child to do; don't name "or else" consequences.** "Stop. Walk with me," a school leader says to a child during morning arrival, instead of "If you don't slow down, you're going to stay in from recess and practice safe walking."

- **Use a neutral, firm, nonaccusatory tone.** A lunch supervisor says to two students, "Mary and Tirza, take a break at the quiet table with Ms. Tang" instead of "Girls, I asked you to use inside voices in the cafeteria. You're screaming across the room to your friends, and that's not allowed here. Do you need to sit at the take-a-break table?"

- **Use as few words as possible.** "Alton, take a break," a teacher says instead of "Alton, take a break. Yelling like that is not acceptable here. We've talked about using kind, friendly words. What's going on for you anyway?" (Although it is important to assert to Alton that yelling is unacceptable and to understand the cause of his behavior, the time for that is later, after Alton has collected himself. In the moment of misbehavior, the briefer the redirection, the more able students are to follow it.)

Show friendly interest in children's home lives

Respecting children's home experiences, traditions, and special interests and giving these a place in school life is important. Such respectful interest allows children to feel valued for who they are and secure enough to take learning risks at school. Help staff see that how they talk to children plays a vital role in this work of honoring students' home cultures.

Encourage staff to listen for bits of information about an activity or interest that families are involved in and reflect it back to the student in casual conversation. For example, consider the first few minutes of the school day. Adults can do so much to help a child feel welcomed and known as a whole person with just a smile and a friendly greeting, accompanied by a quick question that conveys genuine interest in some hobby or event in the child's home life.

"Good Morning, Arjun. What did your family do for the Diwali celebration last night?"

"Hello, Brian. Did you notice any signs of spring during your bus ride? Are your family's daffodils blooming?"

"Good morning, Micah. How are your hip-hop lessons going?"

"Morning, Jody. Did you see any of the Olympics coverage last night? The U.S. hockey team beat out Switzerland!"

"Good morning, Malik. How's your grandmother doing?"

Help staff see the great potential in these small moments and remind them to continue such comments throughout the day.

As a school leader, you can powerfully influence staff to show respectful interest in children's home cultures by modeling it yourself. Make it a priority to see, hear, and learn something about children's lives outside of school (one way to do this is to attend classroom morning meetings), and staff will begin to do the same. If you additionally talk about this topic during staff meetings and in informal conversations, even more staff will follow your lead. The more that school adults know students' home cultures and reflect what they know in their interactions with the children, the more genuinely valued children will feel in school.

Don't overcorrect children's English

Part of respecting children's home culture is respecting the dialect or form of English that they speak at home. Remind school adults that while it's important to teach "standard" English at school, it's also important to balance that teaching with an appreciation for the children's native forms of speech.

As Lisa Delpit points out in *Other People's Children: Cultural Conflict in the Classroom*, if adults constantly correct children's speech, the children may develop negative attitudes toward school. Delpit writes, "Forcing speakers to monitor their language for rules while speaking typically produces silence" (Delpit, 2006, p. 51).

Share with staff a scene from the first moments of a school day. An adult greets a child, saying, "Good morning, Devin. Didn't your team have a ball game yesterday afternoon?" Devin answers, "Good morning, Mr. Williams. I did good. I hit a home run and I run real fast."

Mr. Williams, in that moment, has a decision to make. Ask staff how they might respond if they were Mr. Williams. Would they correct Devin's grammar, or respond to the content of Devin's message?

If their goals in this encounter are to make Devin feel welcome and learn more about what's important in his life, their choice is easy. Suggest that they might respond warmly with something such as "I wish I could have seen that home run and how fast you ran. You must be so proud." This response simultaneously validates Devin's pride in his accomplishment and models more formal conversational English. Later, there would be plenty of opportunities to teach class lessons on correct grammar.

Discuss other scenarios like the one involving Devin. Lead brainstorming and practice of different ways to respond that would simultaneously meet the goals of respecting children's home language and teaching "standard" English.

FINAL THOUGHT

Words Shape How Children See Themselves

Think about a time when someone communicated belief in you in a way that made you form a new vision of yourself. We've all had these moments. Maybe an English teacher helped you imagine yourself as a writer by sharing a timely piece of descriptive feedback. Maybe a coach's encouragement in a particularly tough game helped you muster the courage to keep trying even when the odds seemed insurmountable.

How can we, as school leaders, make sure that the students in our schools are similarly inspired to be the best that they can be? We start by paying attention to our own language, resting everything we say on our belief that all children want to and can do well. Then we make sure that all adults use this kind of language so that it pervades the entire school. If one adult's words and tone can have a profound effect on how one student views himself, think what can happen if all adults at school—from the principal to the custodian—use language that helps children see and become their best selves.

Interactive Modeling

SCHOOL LEADER'S CHECKLIST

❑ **Devote staff meeting time to interactive modeling**

❑ **Make sure all adults agree on behavior expectations**

❑ **Provide interactive modeling scripts**

❑ **Emphasize these to-do's of interactive modeling:**

　❑ Use when there's only one acceptable way (or very few acceptable ways) to do something

　❑ Use intensively early in the year and as needed thereafter

　❑ Model more rather than less

　❑ Give reminders even after careful modeling

　❑ Reinforce positive behavior frequently

　❑ Hold firm to standards

❑ **Use interactive modeling yourself with students**

❑ **Have teachers observe one another's interactive modeling sessions**

Interactive Modeling

Show children how expected behaviors look and sound

Along with positive teacher language, interactive modeling ranks as one of the simplest and most effective tools schools can use for teaching discipline. Many teachers use interactive modeling to teach classroom routines and behaviors, but the technique is highly effective for teaching schoolwide routines and behaviors as well. Through interactive modeling, a technique suitable for all elementary grades, children learn exactly what the behaviors we expect of them look and sound like. So often, children misbehave because they don't understand clearly what's expected or they haven't had sufficient practice in the expected behavior.

Interactive modeling is a technique for providing children with the explicit instruction and practice they need. In interactive modeling, an adult demonstrates a routine—for example, how to carry a chair safely—and asks children to name what she did (looked where she was going, pointed the chair legs down, carried with both hands, and so forth). Then the adult gives the children time to practice while she watches and gives feedback before expecting the children to carry out the behavior independently.

It sounds so simple (and it is), yet we often skip this sort of detailed teaching of routines and expected behaviors, partly because we assume children already know how to carry them out. The fact is that many children—even older elementary students—don't know, or don't know how they're supposed to carry out the routines and behaviors *this year*.

Of all school staff, classroom teachers will be the ones with the greatest need to use interactive modeling, since the job of teaching the rules rests mainly with them. So be sure to help teachers learn to use this technique effectively and expect them to use it liberally.

How to Ensure the Use of Interactive Modeling Throughout the School

The following steps are essential:

- Devote staff meeting time to interactive modeling.

- Make sure all adults agree on behavior expectations.

- Provide interactive modeling scripts.

- Use interactive modeling yourself with students.

- Have teachers observe one another's interactive modeling sessions.

Devote staff meeting time to interactive modeling

Set aside the most time for this early in the year, when the teaching of schoolwide routines and behaviors needs to be the most intense. Be sure to:

- **Show teachers how to use interactive modeling.** Demonstrate the technique or ask a teacher leader to demonstrate it (see pages 67–68 for the steps of interactive modeling and key points to communicate). Ask teachers what they noticed in the demonstration, and then have teachers practice the technique with one another.

- **Decide which routines to model.** Create a list of specific behaviors for teachers to model for each school area (see Chapters 12–15 for sample lists for the playground, cafeteria, hallways, and buses). Also ask recess, lunch, and bus supervisors and classroom teachers which outside-the-classroom routines and behaviors they think are important to focus on with students.

Make sure all adults agree on behavior expectations

If some teachers interpret the playground rule "Play safely on the slide" to mean that walking up the slide is not allowed, whereas others interpret it to mean that walking up the slide is allowed, confusion and discipline problems are likely to result after all these teachers model the rule according to their own interpretations. To avoid such confusion, talk about the specifics of behavior expectations at staff meetings. Drill down to the details. Then post or send written documentation of the shared understanding to all staff.

Provide interactive modeling scripts

Write or lead others in writing scripts for interactive modeling sessions that many staff will be conducting. These scripts can help ensure that everyone is teaching the same expectations and using effective language during modeling sessions. Be sure the scripts have adults using direct, succinct language and naming what to do rather than what not to do (see the right-hand column of the steps of interactive modeling on page 67 for one example of a complete script).

Use interactive modeling yourself with students

As a school leader, you can also use the technique yourself—to teach a recess game, to show the safe way to get on and off the bus, to demonstrate a lunchroom procedure, and so forth. The teacher, observing from the side or joining you in the modeling, can learn from your demonstration, and children may pay extra attention when a school leader models a behavior.

Have teachers observe one another's interactive modeling sessions

Observing colleagues using this technique and debriefing for a few minutes afterward is one of the best ways for teachers to become skillful in its use. Support such observations by creating schedules for teachers to visit one another's rooms and providing classroom coverage for the visiting teacher. You can even cover the classroom yourself. Doing so will send a message of how much you want teachers to use interactive modeling skillfully. Moreover, providing coverage will give you a chance to build relationships with the students in that class.

Good Techniques Enable Good Teaching

Good teaching doesn't just happen. It usually comes from a combination of passion, persistence, and, importantly, having good techniques to use. Interactive modeling is one of those good techniques. In school after school, I see adults using interactive modeling to teach discipline while keeping students engaged and motivated. Lots of times the students thought they were playing—and they were!

Here's an example from the University School of Nashville. A second grade teacher is teaching students how to play tag safely. She starts the lesson in the classroom. The class is gathered in a circle, looking over the school's playground rules:

Play safely and take care of yourself and others.

Rocks, sticks, and sand stay on the ground.

Climb only on the inside of the wooden structure.

Slide down the slide and use stairs for getting to the top.

"If we're going to play safely and take care of others on the playground, how should we be tagging when we play tag?" the teacher asks.

"Don't shove hard when you tag someone," a student says.

"If we're not going to shove hard, what will we do?" the teacher asks.

"We can just tap them softly."

"I'm going to model safe tagging. Pay attention to what I do," the teacher says. With a student volunteer, she demonstrates two safe ways to tag.

"What did you notice?" the teacher asks the class. The class replies that she tapped the student softly on the back and softly on the arm. The teacher then asks two students to demonstrate those safe tagging methods before taking the class outside.

Once outside, the teacher says, "Let's practice what we talked about inside." She divides the children into two groups, one of which is to be the taggers. "Remember, tap softly on the back or arm." She blows a whistle and the children take off running.

A minute later, she blows the whistle again and calls "Circle up!" The students run back quickly (circling up is a routine they've practiced since day one of school), breathing hard, laughing and smiling.

"I noticed a lot of safe tagging," the teacher says. "What did you notice?"

The students are eager to report. "Jonathan just kind of touched me on my arm when he tagged me," one child offers.

"I ran up to Sarah really fast, but I stopped and just tapped her softly," Erica says. Sarah nods with a smile.

"OK, let's practice again. Everyone switch sides." The teacher blows her whistle, and the children begin playing. A minute later she again circles the children up and asks them to report the safe tagging they saw. After a few rounds, she wraps up the practice by saying, "In the next few days I'll be looking for safe tagging like you used today. You look, too, and we'll share our observations." The class then goes back inside, tired but happy.

That's good teaching, made possible by a good technique.

What to Communicate to Teachers About Interactive Modeling

In helping teachers learn interactive modeling, be sure to communicate that they should:

■ Use this technique when there's only one acceptable way (or very few acceptable ways) to do something.

■ Do all the steps (see page 67).

■ Use interactive modeling intensively early in the year and as needed thereafter.

Use this technique when there's only one acceptable way (or very few acceptable ways) to do something

For example, there's only one acceptable way to carry a lunch tray safely. There are only a few safe and friendly ways to tag someone in a tag game. And there's a limited range of acceptable ways to walk down the hall. Let teachers know that these are the types of behavior suitable for interactive modeling.

To teach how to handle situations in which students must draw from a broad repertoire of responses (what to do if they see another student calling someone a name, for example), teachers should use role-playing rather than interactive modeling. (To learn about role-playing, see *Rules in School: Teaching Discipline in the Responsive Classroom*, 2nd edition, 2011, available from www.responsiveclassroom.org.)

Do all the steps

The power of interactive modeling comes from the fact that it not only lets children see exactly what an action should look and sound like, but lets them immediately try out the action under an adult's watchful guidance and receive reinforcing feedback from the adult. Impress upon teachers that to get these benefits, they need to do all steps of an interactive modeling session. These steps are shown at right, illustrated by the example of teaching children how to move through the lunch line. You may want to share this table when you introduce interactive modeling to teachers.

Use interactive modeling intensively early in the year and as needed thereafter

Emphasize that interactive modeling should be used most intensively during the first few weeks of school when teachers are setting expectations and introducing routines. Modeling sessions don't need to be long, but they do need to be frequent. Then, throughout the year, expect teachers to use the technique again whenever they introduce a new routine or activity, whenever children seem to be getting sloppy with a routine and need a reminder, and around vacations and holidays, when children tend to need support to keep their behavior on track.

Interactive Modeling: Moving Through the Lunch Line

Steps	Might Look/Sound Like
1. The adult describes the behavior she or he is about to model.	"When we move through the lunch line, we need to do it safely and considerately. Watch while I demonstrate how to do this."
2. The adult models the behavior.	The adult models *without narrating*. It's best to allow the children to observe for details of the teacher's behavior themselves.
3. The adult asks students what they noticed.	"What did you notice about how I moved safely and considerately?" The children might say "You used both hands to hold your tray" or "You stopped at the door to look around before walking again."
4. The adult asks for one or two student volunteers to model.	"Who else would like to show us how to move through the line safely and considerately?"
5. The adult asks students what they noticed. (Repeat steps 4 and 5 for younger students.)	"What were some ways that Simon moved through the line?" The children name specific safe and considerate behaviors that Simon demonstrated.
6. The class practices.	"Now we're all going to practice moving through the lunch line safely and considerately. I'll be watching to see how you do."
7. The teacher provides feedback.	"You were moving safely and considerately! I saw people watching where they were going, using two hands to hold their trays, and being quiet."

Note: If using interactive modeling to remind students of a routine they've been taught, it's OK to skip the modeling by the adult and go straight to the modeling by student volunteers (step 4).

INTERACTIVE MODELING: TO-DO'S TO HIGHLIGHT FOR TEACHERS

- **Model more rather than less.** It's easy to forget that students may need clarification on something that seems as basic as walking quietly in line. But consider the many reasonable questions that children might have: Do they need to walk single file, or is walking shoulder to shoulder with a friend OK? Is talking OK? How loud? No harm comes from doing too much interactive modeling, whereas harm can come from doing too little. Even if students know a routine, the modeling will be a good reminder.

- **Give reminders even after careful modeling.** It's unrealistic to expect that children will immediately and consistently meet expectations after their teacher models the behaviors once. Just as with academic skills, some children will need reminders and practice before they master behavioral skills. So teachers need to keep giving reminders (for example, before lunchtime, "Remember what we learned about moving safely and considerately through the lunch line") and repeat the interactive modeling if necessary.

- **Reinforce positive behavior frequently.** Students need to hear from us when they carry out a routine or action as we expect them to. Our feedback lets them know that they're on the right track and keeps them motivated to continue the positive behaviors. When giving this reinforcing feedback, be sure to name specific things that the children did—for example, "Wow, class, you lined up so quickly with bodies facing forward and voices off," rather than "Good job lining up." Naming "bodies facing forward and voices off" lets the children know exactly what it is they did well and what to keep doing.

- **Hold firm to standards.** Any time students play a game unsafely, for example, adults should firmly redirect the children to play in the safe way they were taught. When all school adults follow through like this consistently, children get the message that the school is serious about behavior expectations. They're also less likely to be confused about which behaviors are acceptable and which are not.

FINAL THOUGHT

Reinforce, Reinforce, Reinforce

It bears repeating that naming what children are doing well is critical to teaching. Children gain competency by building on their strengths, not their weaknesses, and our naming lets children know their strengths so they can do this building. It also motivates them to keep working hard. Those times when children share recess equipment the way we modeled for them or travel the hallways in the safe, considerate way we demonstrated are valuable teaching moments. A quick word or two at these moments to let children know the specific successful behaviors we saw can powerfully engender more success. So remind teachers often to reinforce, reinforce, reinforce.

Proactive Supports for Students With Challenging Behaviors

❑ **Ensure consistency in discipline among all staff**

  ❑ Provide training to all teachers, paraprofessionals, and interventionists

  ❑ Make sure office staff, bus drivers, cafeteria workers, and custodians know safe and respectful ways to talk to children

❑ **Pay attention to transitions**

  ❑ Offer tips for making transitions feel safe for struggling students

  ❑ Protect time for transitions in teachers' schedules

❑ **Provide students with extra supports for specials, recess, lunch, and the bus**

❑ **Build a schoolwide habit of observing students**

  ❑ Aim for incremental progress

  ❑ Help teachers learn how to adjust assignments as appropriate

❑ **Encourage teachers to build in student reflection time**

❑ **Teach staff to recognize antecedents and to use de-escalation techniques**

❑ **Provide children with social skills instruction outside the classroom**

Proactive Supports for Students With Challenging Behaviors

Ten practices that can help

Anna is a fourth grader with exceptional intellectual potential. But she's preoccupied much of the time in class, seemingly daydreaming. When not daydreaming, she's often disruptive. When she is on task, she's easily distracted by other children. She complains that the work is boring and stupid, or that someone took her paper. When her teacher reminds her of what she's supposed to be doing, Anna acts annoyed, sometimes stomping away and yelling "Leave me alone!"

Her parents report that at home Anna's only focused when watching TV or using the computer, both of which she spends a great deal of time doing. When playing with other children near her home, she often gets into arguments and physical fights.

At school, Anna was deemed ineligible for an Individual Education Plan when tested at the end of third grade. She is being considered for 504 accommodations.

Recently Anna was suspended for a day for a hair-pulling fight in the girl's bathroom, where she had gone without permission to "get even" with someone who had "stolen one of her friends." Several girls in fourth grade

71

report being afraid of Anna, saying she's a bully. The principal has heard from a number of parents about Anna and how she makes it hard for their children to feel safe and to learn well in school.

A Common Story in Our Schools

Children like Anna are not uncommon in our schools. According to the Centers for Disease Control and Prevention, in a recent survey, ten percent of parents of children ages five through seventeen reported that their children had definite or severe difficulties with emotions, concentration, behavior, or getting along with others (Pastor, Reuben, & Loeb, 2009). And of course, bullying continues to be a serious concern in our schools nationwide.

In daily school life, we know that working with students who struggle with behavior requires a disproportionate amount of school adults' time and energy. But the extra investment in helping these children succeed is well worth the effort, because left unaddressed, their behaviors can seriously interfere with their learning as well as the learning of others.

Brian

Brian, a first grader, is another child with behavior challenges. His story is quite different from Anna's but no less common in our schools. Brian was referred for a child study evaluation in kindergarten because of his defiance of adults and physical aggression toward classmates. After the evaluation, Brian was assigned a one-on-one aide. In kindergarten, Brian spit on, hit, bit, and scratched other children and frequently had to be physically restrained by the school interventionist and once by his aide. He had six days of suspension at home that year. Now, in first grade, Brain still has to be restrained frequently when he gets angry because he kicks or punches other children without warning.

Brian's pediatrician has placed him on medication. He has a behavior plan and is rewarded when he can sustain nonaggressive, cooperative behavior for fifteen minutes. His academic performance is still at a preschool level. Other children are cautious around him and do not want to work or play with him unless an adult is present.

Brian enjoys working with his aide but is making slow progress on schoolwork and often has significant difficulty controlling his behavior when he goes to art, music, or computer class. His teacher has talked with the school psychologist to see if Brian might qualify for a self-contained resource room. She's troubled by the lack of safety the other children in the class feel and struck by how different the room feels when Brian is absent.

As for his home life, Brian moved into his grandmother's small apartment during his kindergarten year. His mother is incarcerated, and he has never known a father. He visits his mother in jail and is looking forward to her coming home next year. His grandmother works in a local restaurant as a cook and is worried about losing her job if Brian has to be suspended for any number of days this year. She goes to work early, before school starts, dropping Brian off at her sister's house on the way, but always picks him up at school at the end of the day. Brian loves his Nana and talks about her with his aide all the time.

Ten Practices for Proactively Supporting Struggling Students

As all school leaders know, there are no quick fixes for working with children such as Anna and Brian. The school discipline strategies discussed throughout this book are a crucial foundation, as important to these children as to all others. In addition, however, children who struggle need specialized supports if they and their classmates are to experience success in school. Given the large and growing number of disabilities, disorders, and syndromes typically identified in these children, understanding and identifying all these additionally needed supports is complex work that often requires the expertise of adults in many arenas, possibly including behavior specialists, doctors, and mental health care providers. Addressing this vast and important topic in its entirety is outside the scope of this book.

This chapter, however, discusses ten school practices that provide important general supports to children with challenging behaviors. These ten practices will help any child who's struggling, regardless of the child's diagnosis and what other specialized services the student needs or is receiving. You'll find recommendations for how to lead your school in implementing each practice.

CONTINUED ON PAGE 76

Remembering Children's Need for Safety, Challenge, and Joy

In helping struggling children improve their behavior, keep in mind children's basic need to feel safe, challenged, and joyful. Although it's important for schools to meet these needs when working on discipline with all students, it's especially critical when working with these children.

Safety

In the hierarchy of children's needs at school, safety ranks at the top. Without a sense of basic security, students' ability to think clearly, focus, and engage in normal activities can be seriously impaired.

Ensuring a climate of safety is, of course, one reason we lead efforts to build community at our schools and to establish a positive climate. Instituting the schoolwide use of morning meetings, expecting teachers to instruct their classes in peaceful conflict resolution methods, organizing community-service activities, and the like are all concrete ways to give children a sense of value and belonging and to teach them fairness, civility, and respect. We have firmly in mind the goal of helping children feel safe in school when we launch and sustain such initiatives.

In supporting children's positive behaviors and handling each instance of misbehavior, we must also keep firmly in mind the child's need for safety. This need can be especially strong in struggling children because of their often tenuous ability to manage their emotions and behaviors. For these children, a sense of security usually does not come easily, and they typically require stronger supports than others if they're to be successful.

Challenge

Often, children who struggle with behavior are not being given appropriate academic challenges. Their work is either too easy, which leads to boredom and misbehavior, or too hard, which leads to frustration and anger. When working on discipline with these students, a key is to make sure their work is appropriately challenging for them.

It's also important that we give these children social challenges that are right for them. For example, today's best practices have students doing a great deal of project-based learning with partners or in small groups. But for many children with behavior issues, working with classmates is difficult. So we need to give them extra help and move them incrementally toward independence in working with peers.

Joy

All humans want joy in their lives, and students are no different. Without joy, school feels sterile and dull, and students' learning can be greatly diminished.

Joyful schools are schools filled with excitement, laughter, and a sense of delight. They're also schools with discipline because joy is closely related to self-regulation: When children can focus their attention, control their impulses, persevere, and master skills, they feel more joyful.

For children struggling with behavior, feeling joy at school is especially important because their lives are so often filled with turmoil. In helping these children better regulate their behavior, we're helping them gain a sense of joy in their lives.

The ten practices are:

1. Support positive adult-student relationship building.

2. Ensure consistency in discipline among all staff.

3. Pay attention to transitions.

4. Give students extra supports for specials, recess, lunch, and the bus.

5. Build a schoolwide habit of observing students.

6. Give struggling students lots of positive feedback.

7. Aim for incremental progress in struggling students' work.

8. Encourage teachers to build in student reflection time.

9. Teach staff to recognize antecedents and to use de-escalation techniques.

10. Provide children with social skills instruction outside the classroom.

■ ■ ■

1. Support positive adult-student relationship-building

Positive adult-student relationships are critical to children's success. They help children feel that they belong and are known and valued, and they strengthen children's desire to work hard so they'll do well.

Admittedly, it can be hard to build relationships with struggling students. What may often be lacking between these children and school adults is what psychologists call "attunement." Attunement is key to the development of trust in a parent-child relationship. As Daniel Siegel writes in *The Mindful Brain*,

> When relationships between parent and child are attuned, a child is able to feel felt by a caregiver and has a sense of stability in the present moment. During that here-and-now interaction, the child feels good, connected and loved. The child's internal world is seen with clarity by the parent, and the parent comes to resonate with the child's state. (Siegel, 2007, p. 27)

For children to have a strong, positive relationship with an adult at school, they similarly need to feel a degree of trust in the school adult. But children who struggle with behavior are not always able to trust easily. In some cases, their home relationships may be challenging enough to have compromised their early experience of attunement. Or they're not skilled at reading their teacher's nonverbal cues (facial expression, body language, or subtle tone of voice) to sense the teacher's pleasure or concern. We often call these children "harder to read" and therefore harder to form a strong relationship with, when, in fact, they're having a harder time reading us.

But developing a strong, positive relationship with these children is nonetheless possible—and critical. It's a matter of going slower and persevering.

Our job as school leaders is to create a school culture that values deliberate relationship-building with students. Here are steps you can take:

- **Model it.** Demonstrate relationship-building in your daily interactions with students.

- **Talk about it.** Make adult-student relationship-building a topic of discussion at staff meetings and trainings.

- **Offer concrete tips.** Give staff concrete tips for building relationships with struggling students (see "Building Relationships With Students: Tips to Share With Staff" on page 78).

- **Make time for it.** Give teachers some brief, flexible times away from the activity of the classroom, especially in the early weeks of school, to chat or do a small activity with their harder-to-reach students and build the foundation for lasting trust.

- **Provide trauma information and training.** Help staff learn how to interact with students affected by trauma (see box, "Trauma Training," on page 79).

Relationship-building with students is mostly the province of classroom teachers, since children spend the bulk of their school day with these adults. But paraprofessionals and other staff need to pay attention to this work as well. So often, a student forms a special bond with a nonclassroom adult. That adult may then be a particularly helpful member of a team that provides behavior supports and interventions for the student. So focus your efforts on helping classroom adults build positive relationships with students, but don't neglect other staff.

BUILDING RELATIONSHIPS WITH STUDENTS: TIPS TO SHARE WITH STAFF

■ **Build gradually.** Because struggling children sometimes don't have a lot of positive adult-child experiences to draw upon, they may be unusually cautious about developing new relationships. So it's important to go slow, building day by day through a variety of meaningful verbal and nonverbal interactions, including one-on-one conversations, small instructional groups, and whole-class discussions.

■ **Use the child's name when addressing her.** This is the most basic way of showing warmth and interest in the child. To begin to trust an adult, the child needs to see that the adult actually knows who she is.

■ **Learn the child's interests and mention them to him.** Adults should find out something about what the child likes and wants to be known for and mention what they learn in conversation. Adults might also share something about themselves with the child—some information about their pet or their weekend gardening, for example. As trust builds, the two can have one-on-one conversations to get to know each other further.

■ **Maintain a quiet, firm, friendly tone when redirecting the student.** For children who've experienced trauma, a loud voice, raised in anger or not, may evoke a seemingly out-of-proportion response. When redirecting a student they don't know, adults should respectfully ask the child's name and maintain a quiet, firm, and friendly tone. For example, to a group of rowdy students in the hall, an adult might gently say, "Whoa, looks like you guys are excited to get to recess. Let's see, Brian, Jaden, Malcolm, and—I'm sorry, tell me your name. Wilson?—are you all in Mrs. Abbott's class? Who knows the hallway rules? OK, you can head out. Have fun today, Wilson."

■ **Always transmit empathy and calm.** Even when—in fact, especially when—the child acts out in a forceful way, it's important to show empathy and calm. This is crucial both to the recovery of the misbehaving child and the restoration of calm and order for other students in the vicinity.

2. Ensure consistency in discipline among all staff

Children with behavioral challenges need clear, predictable structures. They need to know who will be teaching and supervising them on any given day, and they need to experience all these adults expecting the same behaviors from them and responding to their behavior mistakes the same way. For students with behavioral challenges, the importance of this consistency cannot be overstated.

Make sure, therefore, to provide training and practice in your school's discipline strategies to all teachers, paraprofessionals, and interventionists who work with these students. In addition, communicate at least key discipline guidelines to everyone else these children may be in contact with. This includes the school secretaries, bus drivers, cafeteria workers, and custodians. Any one of these adults can make or break the child's school experience on any given day.

Begin by teaching all adults safe and de-escalating ways to talk to children with especially challenging behaviors. Explain the power that language has to either calm or escalate negative behaviors. At an absolute minimum, make it clear that the following ways of speaking will not be tolerated:

> **Trauma Training**
>
> For information on working with students affected by trauma, see the following resources:
>
> ■ National Institute for Trauma and Loss in Children
> **www.starrtraining.org/tlc**
>
> ■ National Center for Trauma Informed Care
> **www.samhsa.gov/nctic**
>
> ■ Child Trauma Toolkit for Educators (from the National Child Traumatic Stress Network)
> **www.nctsnet.org**
>
> ■ Child Trauma Academy
> **www.childtrauma.org**
>
> ■ Massachusetts State Trauma Sensitive Schools
> **www.doe.mass.edu/tss**
> (Look for comparable initiatives in your state.)

- ■ Calling to a child from across a room or playground. (Instead, move to the child to speak to him personally.)

- ■ Yelling at any time. (Instead, always maintain a quiet, calm, firm voice.)

- ■ Using sarcasm, mockery, or any derogatory language with a child or a class. (Instead, tell children directly and in a neutral tone of voice what to do.)

(See Chapter 4 for more about positive adult language.)

3. Pay attention to transitions

"Safety first, last, and always" is, rightfully, a mantra in our schools. We carefully practice fire drills, lock-down procedures, evacuations, responses to weather and medical emergencies, and behavioral crisis interventions. We all know that the lives of children and adults depend on highly skilled cooperation in such emergencies.

But for some children, just about every transition in school can feel like an emergency. This can be hard to believe until we see Brian in full melt-down because he didn't know the class was having indoor recess today, or until we hear Anna cursing loudly because no one told her it was time to change into her sneakers for PE.

Considering that the school day is six-and-a-half hours long, with several major transitions—to recess and lunch, to art and PE, to the after-school program—and many small ones such as going into a whole-class meeting or switching from group to independent work, it's no wonder that children like Brian and Anna feel overwhelmed and that the adults teaching them feel exhausted.

Help teachers see that some modest adjustments to their practice can make transition times easier for children with high levels of anxiety—and for themselves. Here are things you can do:

- **Give teachers concrete strategies.** At right are tips for safe transitions that you can pass on to teachers.

- **Facilitate idea exchanges among teachers.** Periodically take a few minutes at staff meetings for teachers to share what worked to help their struggling students through transitions.

- **Fiercely protect time for transitions.** Build unhurried school schedules and signal clearly to teachers that they shouldn't eat into the minutes allotted for transitions in an attempt to cover more content.

MAKING TRANSITIONS SAFE: TIPS TO SHARE WITH TEACHERS

- **Convey understanding and confidence.** Teachers should show struggling children that they understand how difficult transitions are—while also conveying confidence that the students will master transitions and that school will become more fun. And the fact is, students will improve if teachers help them. After focusing on one transition to work on with students, teachers often see carry-over as students apply their learning to other transitions.

- **Do extra modeling and practice.** In addition to using interactive modeling to teach the whole class how to navigate transitions (see Chapter 5), teachers should do additional modeling for individual students as needed.

- **Give a heads-up that a transition is coming.** It's not always easy to stay a step ahead of all transitions, but the more consistently teachers give students a couple minutes' heads-up, the more these children will be able to handle transitions without panicking.

- **Offer a calming activity to do during transitions.** Letting students listen to a short, relaxing piece of music on a headset, go with an adult for a "fresh-air" walk around the building, or do handwork (making a bracelet, beading, finger weaving) can help them stay calm during or around transitions, especially particularly bustling ones. Any small activity that's soothing and that won't distract the other students can be effective.

- **Try allowing a struggling child to help lead transitions.** "Brian, in two minutes it'll be time for the class to line up to go to music. Please give your paper to Ms. Grace. Then I'll give you the chime so you can ring it, and we can let everyone know what's coming next. Do you know what's coming next?" This not only gives the child a heads-up, but sets him up to experience success and allows the rest of the class to see him succeeding.

- **Expect incremental progress.** Teachers should target just a few school transitions for improvement, highlight the child's progress to her, and then build on that success by targeting a few more transitions.

4. Give students extra supports for specials, recess, lunch, and the bus

Some children find it extremely unsettling to be outside the classroom, removed from their classroom routines and their teacher's reassuring presence. Teachers often refer to "dropping off the children" at a special, recess, or lunch. To some children, these times can actually feel like they're being dropped off an emotional cliff.

Teachers cannot be everywhere doing everything, but help them see that they can do the following to support students through times when they won't be there.

- **Explain what they'll be doing when the class is with someone else.** This can be especially reassuring to younger students.

- **Use interactive modeling to teach expected behavior outside of the classroom.** It's best to do this modeling in the actual space—for example, model playground behaviors on the playground and bus behaviors on a bus.

- **Invite other adults to morning meetings.** Teachers can invite special area teachers, playground and cafeteria supervisors, bus supervisors, and bus drivers so the children can get to know these adults in a familiar environment.

- **Prepare children for substitute teachers.** One way is to hold a class meeting to plan everyone's responsibilities on substitute teacher days and then practice those responsibilities before the first such day.

- **Integrate special area activities with classroom learning.** Teachers can talk with the class about what they did in art, for example, and integrate those lessons into classroom work when possible. This helps time outside the classroom feel less removed from classroom life.

- **Give a transferring-in student a tour of school spaces.** Important spaces to cover are the specials classrooms, the playground, and the lunchroom.

Here's what you can do to support classroom teachers with these steps:

■ **Give reminders.** Talk about how important it is to give struggling students extra support for outside-the-classroom time. Give teachers quick reminders at meetings and through notes or staff bulletins.

■ **Provide lists of outside-the-classroom behaviors to teach.** See Chapters 12–15 for sample lists for the playground, cafeteria, hallways, and buses. Consider creating lists for other common spaces in the school. You can ask staff to suggest additions to these lists.

■ **Do some of the teaching yourself.** For example, at the beginning of the year, take classes of children to a particularly challenging place in your school—perhaps the playground or the bus loading area—and introduce that space to the group before teachers start modeling specific behaviors. This deliberate, slow introduction can be especially reassuring for struggling students.

■ **Coordinate a morning meeting visitation schedule.** Be ready to adjust the school schedule on some days to allow for these visitations.

5. Build a schoolwide habit of observing students

Observation is a powerful tool for teaching and for understanding the complex behaviors of children with challenges. It's important that specialists observe and conduct Functional Behavioral Assessments of children. It's equally important that classroom teachers develop the habit and skills of everyday observation. Help teachers see that frequently stepping back for a moment to watch a student like Brian, for example, can allow them to detect patterns such as what tends to trigger his anger, which is critical for helping him get through the day calmly and productively.

To enable teachers to frequently stop and observe, be sure to:

■ **Arrange coverage.** A teacher assistant or you yourself can supervise a class for awhile to free the teacher to step back and observe.

■ **Reassure teachers that observations require only a few minutes.** Even ten minutes of observation on three consecutive days, for example, can be tremendously helpful when a teacher is first getting to know the child.

"After-Teaching"

Once when I was observing in a fifth grade classroom, I noticed the teacher saying quietly to a student, "Walter, move away from Alex and get back to your own work." The teacher then turned her back to help another student with a math problem and next moved to another student who needed help.

Just then, a commotion arose on the other side of the room. The teacher looked up to see Walter and Alex laughing, clearly off-task. The teacher walked over to Walter and said calmly, "Walter, take a break." Walter responded, "What the hell did I do?" at which point the teacher went to the classroom phone and called for the interventionist to come and escort the child from the room.

The teacher's response to Walter's outburst was not inappropriate—it followed the school's discipline protocol. However, a simple strategy that I call "after-teaching" could have prevented the outburst and the need for Walter to leave the room.

After the teacher told him to move away from Alex, Walter, like so many children who lack self-control, was, for a moment, waiting for the teacher's control—waiting to see if she would follow through, whether she meant what she had said.

If the teacher had used this after-teaching moment, she would have turned around to look at Walter once she got to the next student, smiled at Walter, perhaps gestured to reinforce the verbal redirection she'd given him, and waited to see him move to his seat. Only then would she have returned her focus to that next student. Walter would have gotten the message that his teacher's redirection was for real, that she really cared whether he did what she told him to do.

For children with a good deal of self-control, such deliberate after-teaching may not be necessary. These children tend to get, from our initial redirection, that we expect them to do what we said.

Not so for struggling children. With these students, we need to pause long enough to see that they're following through on our teaching. It's as important for principals, lunch and recess staff, and other school adults to do this as it is for classroom teachers. This simple act can turn a child toward expected behavior early on, before a small misbehavior becomes a big one. Then, when the student does what we told them to, we close the learning loop by offering a brief word or a small signal that lets them know we saw, which reinforces the desired behavior.

Will children like Walter sometimes be unresponsive to our after-teaching strategies and require further intervention anyway? Of course.

Does after-teaching significantly decrease the likelihood of this? Does it improve self-control? Does it strengthen the teacher-student relationship? In my experience, yes, yes, and yes.

6. Give struggling students lots of positive feedback

Children who struggle with behavior can never get too much positive reinforcement. As Paula Denton states in her book *The Power of Our Words: Teacher Language That Helps Children Learn*, language "molds our sense of who we are; helps us understand how we think, work, and play; and influences the nature of our relationships" (Denton, 2007, p. 3).

As a school leader, you can influence all staff—especially teachers, with whom children spend the most time—in giving much-needed positive reinforcement to struggling students by frequently reminding them to do so and, importantly, by modeling it yourself.

In guiding staff in this work, emphasize the following:

- **Remember the power of reinforcing language.** Reinforcing positives is so important because it lets students know what they're doing well so they can build on it. (See page 52 of Chapter 4 for to-do's of reinforcing language to pass on to staff.)

- **Mix in nonverbal signals.** Feedback doesn't always have to be verbal. In fact, often, children with challenging behaviors are already overwhelmed by the amount of talk coming their way. A thumbs-up, a bright smile, a wink, or a nod of the head are all messages of affirmation that enable the child to see himself as capable, likeable, and valued.

- **Write children notes.** Children love getting notes from adults. A sticky note on an assignment ("You spelled 'receive' right every time on this paper!"), a folded note on their desk in the morning ("Come see me this morning. I have a surprise for you."), or a note tucked inside a library book ("I found this book about arachnids and checked it out for you.") can do wonders for a child's attitude toward school, especially on a bumpy day.

- **Let classmates see struggling children in a positive light.** During the first few weeks of school, teachers can invite two or three children a day to share something they're "good at." Children who may be accustomed to being noticed only for what they're doing wrong might then tell about being skillful skateboarders, or demonstrate whistling, or share a snack recipe they created. Suggest to teachers that they might dedicate a bulletin board or special shelf to display artifacts of children's strengths.

7. Aim for incremental progress in struggling students' work

Children with behavior issues often have mental discipline or organizational challenges that prevent them from easily absorbing the same quantity or complexity of instruction as their classmates. Such students do best when we chunk up their work and expect them to make progress a little at a time.

Guide teachers on how to do this. Share the following strategies, illustrated by the example of learning to write a friendly letter in third grade:

- **Adjust expectations.** While the majority of the class is expected to practice writing for twenty minutes, the struggling child might be assigned to write one sentence and then show it to the teacher before continuing.

- **Set incremental goals.** On day one, the child is expected to identify whom to write to and think of just one thing to say to that person, with the teacher writing the sentences for him. On a subsequent day, the teacher helps the student think of another thing to tell the letter recipient, staying nearby to scaffold and encourage as the child writes these sentences. On yet another day, the child thinks of and writes, all on his own, some questions to ask the letter recipient, showing his work to the teacher when he's done.

- **Aim for measurable outcomes.** For example, whether the child completed the daily writing tasks is easily measurable by both the teacher and child.

- **Chart success.** Each day that the student completes his letter-writing task, for instance, he might get a check mark on a grid. The concrete, visual representation can be highly motivating to children and is a way for them to reflect on their behavior. (See Practice 8 on page 88 for more on helping students reflect.)

- **Increase the challenge gradually.** Rather than simply being asked to stay on task longer or do greater quantities of work, the struggling child should also be given more complex and interesting tasks. This lets him feel competent and can increase motivation over time. For example, as the child shows readiness, he might have the choice of adding a drawing or map to his letter, along with an explanatory sentence. Of course, it's important that teachers provide help so children will succeed as they're given more challenges.

- **Find ways for the class to acknowledge the child's work.** It's vital, for example, that the student have a turn reading his finished letter aloud just like the rest of the class or have an equal spot in author circles, project displays, and work sharings.

Helping individual students in this way while meeting the needs of the rest of the class is challenging work. Here are just a few ways you can help:

- **Keep encouraging teachers.** Your encouragement means so much to teachers. Continually recognize their patience and diligence.

- **Provide professional development.** Provide staff with training, books, articles, DVDs, and group discussions on individualizing work for struggling students.

- **Advocate for staffing.** Work toward having enough behavior specialists and instructional aides on staff to help provide students with the individualized attention they need.

- **Visit classrooms to connect personally with struggling students.** It matters when you visit. It makes a big impression on these children when their principal or another school leader comes into the classroom and privately acknowledges their accomplishments by asking, for example, to see their progress notebook or other success-tracking system.

8. Encourage teachers to build in student reflection time

Time for reflection in school too often disappears in the busyness of the school day. Yet some of the deepest learning occurs when, at the end of a lesson, activity, or challenging social situation, students are given time to reflect rather than quickly moved on to the next thing. Over the course of a year, these brief moments can add up to hundreds of golden opportunities to cultivate student understanding and transformation.

Like all children, children who struggle with behavior have an innate ability to reflect on their learning. But because these children often have problems paying attention, educators can sometimes be quick to dismiss their aptitude. Yet reflection can be the very thing that helps these children develop much-needed social and emotional skills. Daniel Siegel, arguing that reflection should be the 4th R in education, writes that "reflective skills harness our prefrontal capacity for executive attention, prosocial behavior, empathy and self-regulation" (Siegel, 2007, p. 262).

You can support teachers in guiding students to reflect on their learning and behavior by encouraging them to use these simple, effective methods:

- **Close each lesson by asking a think-back question.** It's OK—in fact it's important—for teachers to take these few minutes before transitioning to the next activity. Possible questions include:

  - What was the most important idea for you in this (story, piece of writing, math lesson)?

  - Why do you think we changed our partners in reading today?

  - What is something you might share with your family tonight about what you learned in science today?

  - Who remembers what our goal for this lesson was? Did we reach it?

■ **End each school day with a closing circle.** The class gathers in a circle for five to ten minutes before dismissal. The teacher asks the children to share one of these:

◆ Something they're proud of from that day

◆ One thing they want to work more on the next day

◆ Something they did to help someone that day

◆ One thing the whole class can be proud of

◆ What a character in a book they're reading might be up to the next day

(For more about closing circles, see "Closing Circle: A Simple, Joyful Way to End the Day" by Dana Lynn Januszka and Kristen Vincent, *Responsive Classroom Newsletter*, February 2011, www.responsiveclassroom.org.)

■ **Check in privately with individual children at the end of the day.** Children who are having a hard time with behavior especially benefit from such check-ins. Teachers should ask specific reflection questions such as the closing circle ones listed above rather than general questions such as "How was your day?" (It's also highly effective for school leaders to come to the classroom to do this check-in with struggling students.)

■ **Take five minutes to talk after the class returns from a special.** Before moving on to the next subject, the teacher asks the children to name things they did or learned in that special. Teachers can do a similar five-minute check-in after morning arrival, the midday recess and lunch break, and an all-school meeting.

9. Teach staff to recognize antecedents and to use de-escalation techniques

Adults in school are often surprised when a child's behavior erupts "suddenly." Almost always, however, these behaviors aren't actually sudden. They're preceded by signs that, if we're looking, tell us an explosion is about to come. If we recognize these antecedents, we'll have a chance to de-escalate the tension and prevent the explosion.

To help staff learn to recognize antecedents and use de-escalation techniques:

- **Dedicate staff meeting time to this topic.** Share the de-escalation techniques below with them. Look into bringing in an expert on the topic to give a talk or workshop. Guide staff in role-playing challenging situations with each other.

- **Put it in the staff handbook.** Include information, such as the tips below and key points from de-escalation training, in this resource so staff can review it easily.

- **Make cheat sheets for staff.** Print critical de-escalation steps on cards that staff can post in convenient spots as reminders.

- **Make sure all staff know the procedure for activating the crisis team.** Communicate clearly and often when staff should alert the crisis team and the procedures for doing so (see Chapter 9).

DE-ESCALATION TECHNIQUES TO SHARE WITH STAFF

- **Look for physical signs of tension.** Children often give physical clues that they're about to explode. Look for children balling their fists, holding their breath, drumming their fingers, pacing, and the like.

- **Try a soothing, simple redirection at this point.** Right when a child is showing signs of stress, try to bring down the tension by saying in a calm, soothing voice, "Here, squeeze this, Brian" while handing Brian a ball to squeeze, or "Anna, try taking a few deep breaths. I'll breathe with you for a few minutes."

- **Give the child space if a calm redirection doesn't work.** If the child is already too agitated or if the child's tension mounts, do the following:

  - *Stay at a comfortable distance.* Sense what distance is comfortable for the particular child. For some children, closer is more comfortable, but for others, it causes more anxiety. If in doubt, err on the side of keeping a greater distance to prevent the child from feeling threatened.

- ✦ ***In general, avoid eye contact.*** Asking an upset child to look at us can ratchet up their anxiety.

- ✦ ***Talk slowly and quietly.*** It's crucial to do this even if we don't feel calm. Children react sensitively to our tone of voice. Deliberately slowing down our speech can have a soothing effect on a child whose anxiety or upset is escalating.

- ✦ ***Never take what the child is saying personally.*** The child's explosion is not about us. An upset child, like an upset adult, will often say things that she doesn't mean.

- ■ **Get help.** Whatever intervention is tried, if it's not successful and the child is quickly losing control, it's imperative to get immediate assistance. Use the school's protocol for handling these situations. It is never a sign of weakness to ask for help. It is, rather, a sign of being responsible.

A word about take-a-break (positive time-out) for children under stress: Help adults understand that although it can sometimes be effective to have a child go to take-a-break when she's just beginning to be agitated, doing so can also escalate the agitation. Staff members will have to use their judgment. They may have a take-a-break protocol that's effective for most children, but it's OK, and likely necessary, to deviate from it for children with challenging behaviors. (For information about in-classroom take-a-break, see *Rules in School: Teaching Discipline in the Responsive Classroom*, 2nd edition, 2011, available at www.responsiveclassroom.org. For information about out-of-classroom take-a-break, see Chapter 10 of this book.)

10. Provide children with social skills instruction outside the classroom

Social skills lessons in the classroom benefit children with challenging behaviors enormously, just as they benefit all students. But these children typically also need additional small group or one-on-one instruction outside the classroom. This additional social skills instruction, best provided by counselors, speech and language therapists, school social workers, and psychologists, should be built into students' Individual Educational Plans or 504s with the same degree of specificity that we might see for academic interventions.

Finding the right intervention for your school or a particular child you're working with can require some work—there are as many programs for social skills instruction as there are for addressing students' reading or math challenges. These national clearinghouses can lead you to credible programs:

- Technical Assistance Center on Social Emotional Intervention (www.challengingbehavior.org)

- National Dissemination Center for Children with Disabilities (www.nichcy.org)

- Child Development Institute (www.childdevelopmentinfo.com)

- Wrightslaw (www.wrightslaw.com)

- American Academy of Child and Adolescent Psychiatry (www.aacap.org)

- Center for Effective Collaboration and Practice (http://cecp.air.org)

Regardless of which approach your school chooses, remember these essentials:

- **Clearly define the intervention.** School leaders should lead in clearly defining the additional social skills training that's right for the school.

- **Advocate tirelessly.** School leaders need to keep speaking out and pushing for social skills services for struggling students. This includes making sure child study meetings include appropriate specialists who are conversant with best practices for social skills instruction.

- **Measure and report progress.** Whatever social skills programs your school chooses, make sure it allows for the setting of clear, measurable goals and includes mechanisms for reporting progress. We expect these elements for academic interventions. We should expect no less for social skills interventions.

- **Allot time.** Provide time for classroom teachers to meet regularly with the school adults who are providing the additional outside-the-classroom instruction to struggling children. This ensures continuity and consistency between the child's lessons inside and outside the classroom, and it encourages school adults to support each other in the challenging work of teaching struggling children.

■ **Be accountable.** We must hold ourselves and our schools just as accountable for providing students the extra social skills instruction they need as for providing the extra math and reading supports they need.

CHIP REFLECTS

On the Child's Side

One of the most important things I've learned as a school leader is that when a student has a persistent behavior problem, what works to restore positive behavior is to get on the child's side and search together for a solution.

Admittedly, it's all too easy to slip into an oppositional stance. Especially when we have too much on our minds, we're tempted to use the "because I'm the principal" approach, demanding respect. I've been there. I've had days when I've wanted to *make* a student behave a certain way.

These are not our shining leadership moments, but they happen. These are times to call on a fellow administrator or a counselor to take the student while we gather ourselves for a few minutes—to have our own take-a-break, if you will.

Then, when we return to the student in a calm state, we can use the *Responsive Classroom* problem-solving conference technique for getting on the child's side to look for solutions. Many teachers use this strategy successfully in classrooms. Here's an adapted version for use by school leaders:

◆ **Talking at a calm time.** I make sure the child and I, myself, have calmed down before beginning any problem-solving.

◆ **Noting positive things about the student.** "I notice you've been playing in a friendly way with other kids at recess. And you've been eating with some new kids at lunch." This establishes a positive tone for the conversation.

✦ **Asking the student's view of what happened.** "Tell me what happened at lunch today."

✦ **Describing objectively what I know about the incident.** "I heard that when you and your tablemates disagreed about washing the table, you yelled at them. Then when Ms. Monroe told you to take a break, you threw your book at her."

✦ **Asking the student what she or he noticed.** "What else did you notice about what happened?"

✦ **Stating the need to solve the problem and inviting the student to work with me on it.** "It's important that we find a way for you to handle stuff like this peacefully even when you're angry. Would you like to work together on that?" (If the student says no, I stop the conversation and look for another way to handle the problem. There's no use forcing a student to collaborate with us.)

✦ **Seeing if the child has ideas about what caused the misbehavior.** "Why do you think this happened?" Often children have a hard time articulating the cause. So I use nonjudgmental "Could it be?" language to offer some real possibilities. "Could it be that you were still angry about something that happened at recess? Could it be that when people disagree with you, you get so angry you forget to use kind words?"

✦ **Together, thinking of two or three ways to prevent a similar problem in the future.** These ideas will flow from what the child identified as the cause of the misbehavior. Perhaps an idea is that if the child is angry, he'll ask a teacher for help. Or he'll take his turn at table washing for the time being, and then tell a teacher or me later if he feels the matter was unfair.

✦ **Agreeing on one idea to try.** I guide the child in picking one of the solutions. I then tell the student that I'll inform his teacher and parents about our plan and check back on his progress later.

(For more about *Responsive Classroom* problem-solving conferences, see *Solving Thorny Behavior Problems: How Teachers and Students Can Work Together* by Caltha Crowe, 2009, and *Teaching Children to Care: Classroom Management for Ethical and Academic Growth, K–8*, revised edition, by Ruth Sidney Charney, 2002. Both are available from www.responsiveclassroom.org.)

FINAL THOUGHT

"Welcome Back!"

One of the most important things school leaders can do to support students is to warmly welcome them back into the school after they've needed to leave for behavioral reasons. Students often feel highly vulnerable in this moment of return and can suddenly be overcome with embarrassment, doubt, anger, or shame. Being welcomed by you and gently eased into the activities under way can help relieve these feelings and greatly increase the child's chances of success. "Welcome back, Brian. I'm so glad to see you in school this morning," the principal says when Brian returns after an at-home suspension. "I know you can follow our school rule about being kind to others. I've seen you smiling and saying 'thank you'. I'll check in with you later to see how things are going."

Teachers must also value forgiveness and practice it. "Welcome back, Anna. We're on page thirty-four in our math book. I'll check in with you in a minute," Anna's teacher says when Anna comes back from a take-a-break outside the classroom.

Regardless of how long the student has been gone and what happened before the child left, a genuine and robust "Welcome back" should always be our first response upon the child's return. In this way, we convey our conviction that the child is worthy and capable. We convey that we have clear expectations of the student and are ready to offer specific supports. This is how school should be for Brian and Anna and for all children.

School-Home Partnerships

SCHOOL LEADER'S CHECKLIST

❑ **Make school an inviting place for all families**

- ❑ Think about families with limited English abilities
- ❑ Create a welcoming physical environment
- ❑ Greet families warmly when they come to school
- ❑ Provide flexible meeting times
- ❑ Consider holding meetings off school grounds
- ❑ Offer friendly, low-pressure events

❑ **Build trusting relationships with parents**

- ❑ Examine your school's beliefs about parents
- ❑ Send a welcome letter to parents before or right when school starts
- ❑ Keep reaching out all year long
- ❑ Consider holding parent conferences during the first weeks of school

❑ **Explain the school's discipline approach to parents**

- ❑ Help parents understand what's positive about the approach
- ❑ Use formal (for example, parent handbook) and informal (for example, parent coffees and short articles in the school newsletter) methods of communication

❑ **Expect teachers to communicate with parents regularly about discipline, especially before problems arise**

CHAPTER 7

School-Home Partnerships

Bring parents into the conversation about discipline

One evening soon after school started in the fall, a large group of kindergarten parents are gathered at school for a parent meeting. They've been informed that the theme of the meeting will be "positive discipline," and many are eager to learn what the school means by that.

Many of the parents are surprised to find the chairs arranged in a circle. Others seem pleased by an unexpected question in the welcome message that a school leader has posted:

Welcome, Parents!

This evening we will examine some different approaches to discipline and share some of our hopes and goals for our children. Be thinking about how you would respond to the following:

If you could teach your child one idea, just one, that they would carry with them for the rest of their lives, what would that idea be?

■ ■ ■

The positive discipline theme, the chairs in a circle, and the question all add up to giving the parents an important first impression: This school wants to support my child, values community, and cares about what I want for my child.

Communicating with parents about discipline has to be a part of any school's discipline work, and leading such communication is a crucial task of a school leader. Children have the greatest chance of reaching their potential and becoming positive members of the school community if schools treat parents as partners in discipline work. This partnership hinges on good communication. The more informed and heard parents are, the more effectively they can work with your school to support their children's behavior.

This chapter discusses four important actions you should take in forming a partnership with parents around discipline:

- Make school an inviting place for all families.

- Build trusting relationships with parents.

- Explain your school's discipline approach to parents.

- Expect teachers to communicate with parents about discipline.

Make School an Inviting Place for All Families

One of the most basic yet important steps for school leaders is to make school a place that families want to come to and be involved with. School may be a familiar and comfortable place for us educators, but it can feel the opposite for some families. For many parents, past negative experiences with school may linger like "ghosts in the classroom," as Sara Lawrence-Lightfoot puts it. Their feelings toward school and their interactions with school adults are "shaped by their own autobiographical stories ... often-unconscious replays of childhood experiences in families and in school" (Lawrence-Lightfoot, 2003, pp. 3–4).

About the term "parent"

Students come from a variety of homes with a variety of family structures. Many children are being raised by grandparents, other relatives, siblings, or foster parents. This book uses the word "parent" to refer to and honor anyone who is the child's primary caregiver.

As a school leader, be aware that parents may have these negative past experiences and take deliberate steps to make school feel welcoming and safe for all families. Here are some ways:

Honor all family structures

Think about all the families in your school. Does your communication include all family structures (single parents, grandparents raising children, parents living together, separated parents sharing custody, same-gender parents, different-gender parents, stepfamilies, foster parents, and so on)? Check for salutations in letters, wording used in school forms, and even the way school adults talk to students about their parents ("your mom and dad" versus "your parents," "your family," or even "an adult who takes care of you," for example) to make sure you're not inadvertently excluding some members of your community.

Think about families with limited English abilities

Make sure signs throughout the school are easy to understand for families who don't speak English well. Get parent letters translated into languages they're more comfortable with. And have translators available during parent conferences and meetings.

If your district doesn't have a system for providing these translations, think about whether any of your school's staff, perhaps an ELL teacher, can serve as a translator. Then free that person up to come to conferences or meetings with parents. Or look among the parents for translation expertise and ask if they're able to help out.

Create a welcoming physical environment

Walking through the front doors of a school should allow families to get the message "Everyone is welcome here." Begin by making sure the main entrance is clearly marked. Put up a welcoming message to visitors near the door. Display student work or photos of students so families can see their student represented. Make sure the office is clean and uncluttered. Have adult-sized chairs in the waiting area.

At the Learning Community Charter School in Central Falls, Rhode Island, parents and visitors are even greeted by fresh-brewed coffee, the daily newspaper, and café tables and chairs in the lobby area. Not every school needs to provide coffee and newspapers; the point is to make sure the physical space is clean, comfortable, and cheerful.

Greet families warmly when they come to school

The most welcoming physical environment can go only so far, though, without a warm and friendly personal connection. At Sarasota Suncoast Academy in Sarasota, Florida, the principal and office staff start the day outside the building, greeting students and parents one by one as they arrive. At Dame School in Concord, New Hampshire, school adults station themselves along the hallways each morning, greeting students and any accompanying family members as they arrive (see pages 211–212 in Chapter 14 for more about Dame School). You can institute similar setups to ensure that families receive a warm, welcoming greeting when they come to your school.

Provide flexible meeting times

To accommodate parents' work schedules, try to offer different times of day for them to meet with school staff. For example, the Learning Community Charter School mentioned above offers twice-monthly open parent meetings—one in the morning and one in the evening—when parents can drop in to the co-directors' office to share concerns and ideas. Whenever possible, provide free child care during evening gatherings to make parent attendance even more possible.

Also create schedules and other accommodations to allow classroom teachers to hold parent conferences and classroom family events at flexible times.

Consider holding meetings off school grounds

Consider meeting with parents at community centers, places of worship, libraries, or even restaurants in their communities. Encourage teachers to do the same. Not only will this help those who have limited transportation, but the meetings may feel less intimidating for some parents if they take place in familiar settings in their own neighborhood.

Offer friendly, low-pressure family events

Think about holding schoolwide parent breakfasts, family picnics, family literacy or math activity nights, and other such events that allow parents to feel known, befriend other families, and draw closer to school. To keep these events low-pressure for parents, make activities a choice rather than a have-to. For example, invite but don't require parents to share something about themselves or their families. Allow parents to try an activity that their children do at school—writing a poem or playing a recess game, for instance—but make it perfectly fine for them to pass on the activity.

Make information easily available to parents

As a first step, regularly post communications to parents and relevant links for them on your school's website. In addition, if you can, create a family resource room in your school, a welcoming space that's open to parents throughout the day. Organize a few staff members to furnish this space with materials that help parents support their children's school success.

For example, there might be a bulletin board, free brochures, and a check-out system for books and DVDs on topics ranging from child development and curricular initiatives to community resources that support children's well-being. There could even be learning activity kits that parents can borrow and use with their children at home. If you can't set up a dedicated resource room, put parent materials in the lobby, office, or any other school space that parents frequent.

Build Trusting Relationships With Parents

A trusting relationship is a prerequisite to schools and parents working together on discipline. Although the day-to-day building of school-home relationships is primarily the province of teachers, school leaders play the crucial role of developing a culture in which this work is seen as a priority. Here are important ways to build this culture.

Examine your school's beliefs about parents

Tune in to how the adults at your school talk about students' families and how they act toward them. Does everyone at school believe that all parents want the best academically and socially for their children? Does everyone believe that the school has much to learn from parents about how best to teach their children? Does everyone believe in celebrating families' diverse backgrounds and cultures?

In easy and trying times—especially in trying times—deliberately address staff's beliefs about families by holding conversations on the topic in staff meetings and reminding them of parents' positive intentions for their children. Most importantly, model respect for parents yourself by always showing it in your speech and actions.

CONTINUED ON PAGE 104

Sample Overview of Discipline

(in a parent handbook)

_____ School uses the *Responsive School* Discipline approach. The goals of this approach are to ensure that children:

- Feel physically and emotionally safe in school so that they can learn at their best.

- Learn the skills for working and learning cooperatively with others.

Our schoolwide rules are:

Work hard and allow others to work hard.
Listen carefully and speak kindly.
Take care of school property.

The adults at _____ School take time to model and teach children how to translate these rules into action in different situations. At the beginning of the year, we introduce rules and behavior expectations and guide students in practicing them. Using respectful words and tones of voice, we remind children of these expectations. When children behave positively, we let them know that we noticed. These actions let children know what the expectations are and help them stay motivated to meet those expectations.

When children misbehave, the adults at school handle the misbehavior firmly while preserving the child's dignity. Our first step is to stop the misbehavior quickly and simply (for example, with a brief word or gesture). If needed, we take further steps to help the child regain self-control, fix any problems caused by his or her mistake, and get back to productive learning.

In deciding how to handle students' misbehavior, we take into account how severe the misbehavior is and how likely it is to happen again. We may:

- Simply give a reminder or tell the child to do something different.

- Have the child sit closer to the teacher or other adult (often just being closer to an adult helps children remember what they're supposed to do).

- Use "take-a-break" (the child goes to a distraction-free space in the room for a little while to regain self-control).

- Limit the child's choice of activities for awhile (for example, blacktop games only at today's recess; try field games again tomorrow).

- Guide the child in fixing problems caused by his or her mistake (for example, helping the custodian clean up if she or he made a mess in the bathroom).

When a student needs additional supports, we may:

- Use buddy teacher take-a-break (the child goes to a distraction-free space in another teacher's room for awhile to regain self-control).

- Use private take-a-break (the child goes to a supervised nonclassroom place, such as the counselor's office, for awhile to regain self-control).

- Have the child stay for a longer period of time in the supervised place (in-school suspension).

- Have the child spend a period of time at home (at-home suspension).

- Meet with the child and/or parents to find other solutions.

When a child is asked to stay home from school, a parent must accompany the child to school the next day for a re-entry meeting with the teacher and an administrator. This meeting is typically held within the first hour of the day.

We at _____ School strongly believe that children want to and can meet expectations. We value partnering with parents to help students do well in school and feel good about going to school.

Send a letter to parents before or right when school starts

Reach out with a letter from the principal or similar communication that welcomes families into the school community and conveys that your school cares about their child's success.

Encourage teachers to send similar notes to their students' parents. In their notes, teachers might additionally invite parents to share a few insights about their child. Make this easy for teachers to do by supplying them with ready-made postcards or notecards that they can customize. (See *Parents and Teachers Working Together* by Carol Davis and Alice Yang, 2005, available at www.responsiveclassroom.org, for sample teacher letters and other parent communication tips to share with your staff.)

Keep reaching out all year long

Throughout the year, continue to send principal's letters to parents from time to time. A main point of these communications is to continue showing parents that your school cares about their child and to keep open a line of communication with them. Highlight academic and social skills successes achieved by the student body as a whole. Tell about schoolwide activities designed to support further academic and social growth. And always extend an invitation to parents to share their opinions and concerns.

In addition, expect teachers to keep reaching out to parents throughout the year as well—with quick phone calls or brief notes to tell parents of a contribution or a strength that they observed in the child and to invite parent input. Again, ease the note-writing by supplying teachers with notecards or postcards that they can customize.

Consider holding parent conferences during the first weeks of school

Another way to show parents that they matter is to hold the first parent conferences at the start of school, rather than in November. Instruct teachers that their goal in this early conference is to start building a relationship and to gather information that could help them teach the student well. They might ask parents to share their hopes for their child's year, what their child likes or is good at, how their child learns best, and any family hobbies or skills the parents might like to share with the class.

Listen to parents

The importance of this cannot be overstated. Whenever you meet with parents, make it a point to listen more than you talk. Advise teachers to do the same. And don't forget the time-honored suggestion box. Place a few at key locations throughout the building (front lobby, main office, family resource room, and so forth). Parents will then have a low-pressure way to communicate their ideas and concerns. When school adults listen, parents feel respected and known, and the school gets important information. Good listening paves the way for successful school-home collaboration on discipline issues.

Explain Your School's Discipline Approach to Parents

The more clearly parents understand the school's approach to discipline, the more fully they can help support positive school behavior in their children. Here are important things to remember when you explain your school's discipline approach.

Use formal and informal methods of communication

Publish an overview of your school's approach to discipline in the parent handbook (see pages 102–103 for a sample overview). Also periodically highlight key aspects of your school's discipline work at PTA/PTO meetings.

In addition, look for less formal opportunities throughout the year to communicate this information. For example, Matt Miller, principal of Roundtown Elementary in York, Pennsylvania, holds parent coffees that focus on different aspects of school discipline. You can also write short articles about discipline in your school newsletter (see sample on page 107).

Varying your means of communication prevents parents from experiencing information overload and allows you to reach parents with different preferred ways of receiving information.

EXPLAIN WHAT'S "POSITIVE" ABOUT YOUR SCHOOL'S APPROACH

Describe for parents:

- **How school adults teach expected behaviors.** Name the goals of your school's discipline approach and its schoolwide rules. Then highlight the practices that school adults use to support children in choosing and maintaining positive behaviors—for example, their use of interactive modeling and positive language to help children translate rules into action and their community-building practices in classrooms and schoolwide.

- **How school adults respond to misbehavior.** Chapter 9 explains how important it is to establish a clear set of positive responses to misbehavior for all staff to use. Give parents an overview of your school's responses, emphasizing their positive nature. Stress that the immediate goal is to stop the misbehavior so that the learning environment can remain safe and supportive of every student's best learning. Explain that any follow-up procedures are aimed not at punishing the student but at helping the student regain composure, repair any damage done, and return to productive learning. Emphasize that preserving the child's dignity is a top priority.

Expect Teachers to Communicate with Parents About Discipline

After giving parents an overview of your school's discipline approach, expect teachers to follow up with details of discipline practices in their classrooms. For example, advise them to describe for parents:

- The classroom rules and the process of generating them

- How they teach expected behaviors in various classroom situations

- How they teach expected recess, lunch, hallway, and bus behaviors

- Methods they've taught students for calming down and regaining self-control when upset

- What take-a-break (positive time-out) looks like in their classroom

CONTINUED ON PAGE 108

Sample Principal's Article About Discipline
(in a school newsletter)

This week marks our first full month of school. Our community morning meeting on Thursday will focus on our schoolwide rules:

■ Do your best learning and help others do their best learning.

■ Take care of yourself and others.

■ Keep our school clean and green.

We have been teaching and helping students practice these rules throughout the building and will continue to do so all year. Teachers are talking with children about what these rules should look like and sound like at arrival time, in the hallways, at lunch and recess, and during all-school gatherings. Classes are making banners that show these behaviors and will be sharing these banners during our community morning meeting on Thursday. You are welcome to join us for this celebration!

As parents, you can help your child understand and follow the schoolwide rules by talking about them often. Some questions to ask your child are:

■ How did you do with following the rules at recess (or lunch, all-school meeting, etc.) today?

■ What did you do, or see others do, at school today to keep the school clean and green?

■ Which of the schoolwide rules is hardest for you to follow?

■ What do your classmates do that helps you do your best learning?

To help us all live up to our "keep our school clean and green" rule, the school will be starting a recycling program called "Dream Green." We will share ideas about it with students on Thursday. Be sure to ask your child about this!

- Who their buddy teacher is and what buddy teacher take-a-break looks like

These details help parents picture the day-to-day teaching and reinforcing of positive behavior at their child's school and see how schoolwide and classroom discipline go hand in hand.

Support teachers in using a variety of formats when communicating with parents. Here are just a few ideas:

- Encourage teachers to send home classroom newsletters.

- Set up a way to record classroom newsletters so parents can call to listen to them.

- Expect teachers to talk about discipline during back-to-school nights.

- Set up classroom websites where teachers can post messages to parents about discipline and other topics.

BABS REFLECTS

District and School Policies: Sometimes a Balancing Act

What do we do when our school's beliefs and district's policies on discipline don't align perfectly? My colleague Karen Casto, a former administrator, sometimes found herself in this situation while serving as principal of Penn Valley Elementary School in Levittown, Pennsylvania. One time, for example, the district policy required that the school impose a suspension for a child's behavior. It was not the intervention that Karen felt the child needed. Her dilemma was how to respect the requirements of the district and also meet the needs of the child—and then how to explain the situation to the child's parent. She told the parent, "I don't have a choice about our immediate response, but our school very much wants to work with you to help your child develop other strategies for handling this issue. That's the important work as we go forward."

Together with the parent, the school came up with some strategies the child could use to monitor and regulate her own behavior, including using a stress ball and going to a special place in the classroom to re-group when needed. The teacher and guidance counselor checked in daily with the student to see how the strategies were working. In addition, the student and teacher together named positive target behaviors, which all of the child's teachers looked for and consistently reinforced.

From time to time, all school leaders have to strike a delicate balance between differing beliefs and policies that our schools must answer to. Successfully finding that balance requires being practical while never losing sight of the child's needs and communicating honestly and respectfully with the parent.

FINAL THOUGHT

Research Backs Up What We Know

The National Coalition for Parent Involvement in Education cites overwhelming research that says family involvement in education is crucial. Students with "involved parents, no matter what their income or background," it says, are more likely to:

- Have higher grades and test scores

- Attend school regularly

- Have better social skills

- Show improved behavior

- Adapt well to school

(National Coalition for Parent Involvement in Education, n.d.)

Of course educators know the benefits of parent involvement from their own experience and instinct. But now we have a growing body of research that says this is true. The case for parental involvement is solid. The rest is up to us.

Staff Learning Together

SCHOOL LEADER'S CHECKLIST

❑ **Plan how to include all staff in learning about discipline**

    ❑ Teachers

    ❑ Paraprofessionals

    ❑ Other school adults, including office staff, custodians, and bus drivers

❑ **Devote staff meeting time to discipline issues** (all-staff meetings, grade-level planning meetings, cross-grade learning structures or networks)

❑ **Plan which discipline topics to focus on**

    ❑ Positive adult language and interactive modeling

    ❑ Any specific areas of focus (for example, cafeteria discipline) in your school

    ❑ Topics requested by staff: _____

❑ **Make the learning effective for adults**

    ❑ Establish a tone of respect

    ❑ Offer some choice

    ❑ Provide practical solutions

    ❑ Choose appropriate conversation structures

    ❑ Cultivate a habit of reflection

❑ **Structure colleague observations and small-group conversations**

CHAPTER 8

Staff Learning Together

Deepen skills around discipline

Consistency among school adults is a key to effective discipline throughout the school. Given that fact, a priority for school leaders must be to provide ample opportunity for staff to learn together about discipline.

It's not enough that staff know the school's discipline policies. They need to continuously talk with each other about ways to put these policies into action. And they need to practice these ways with each other. Here's why:

First, such learning-focused contact among teachers, specialists, lunch and recess supervisors, and all other school staff helps ensure that all these adults are on the same page. It's through discussion, group practice and role-plays, observations and debriefings, and similar experiences that staff really learn the details of the school's discipline policies and practices. And it's the details that can make or break adults' interactions with children around discipline.

Second, adults—like children—learn best through social interaction. Adults will understand discipline strategies more deeply and hone their skills more sharply if they have opportunities to learn with their colleagues.

Make sure your staff learn together about discipline frequently and throughout the year—not just during workshops and trainings, but between them as well; not just during the creation of schoolwide rules, but also in the weeks and months afterward; and, very importantly, not just when children are showing behavior problems, but even when there isn't a problem at hand that needs solving. It's this day-to-day collaborative learning among staff that drives school discipline to new heights.

This chapter recommends the following important leadership actions for putting this kind of ongoing adult learning in place at your school:

- Plan how to include all staff in learning about discipline.

- Devote staff meeting time to discipline issues.

- Plan which discipline topics to focus on.

- Delve into the details.

- Structure colleague observations and small-group conversations.

Plan How to Include All Staff in Learning About Discipline

All staff don't have to be in the same meetings or trainings together—schedules and other constraints often don't allow that—but all should have opportunities, in large groups or small, to learn with colleagues about discipline. Think about the adult gatherings already going on at your school: staff meetings, grade-level meetings, professional development days, and so forth. How can you use parts of these to focus on discipline? Whom do these existing meetings leave out? Think especially about paraprofessionals. Do you need to create new meetings or trainings for these adults? If you're going to have a special training or practice session on discipline practices, can you have teachers and paraprofessionals in the same session? This last idea, if you can work it out schedule-wise, can help the whole staff feel like they're on the same team.

Devote Staff Meeting Time to Discipline Issues

Most schools have regular all-staff meetings, grade-level planning meetings, and cross-grade learning structures or networks. Regardless of what other structures you create for staff to learn together, at least use parts of these meetings to discuss and practice discipline strategies. For example, some all-staff meeting time may be devoted to the use of positive language, and some grade-level meeting time may be used to discuss how to remind children to follow schoolwide rules during an upcoming grade-wide activity.

Plan Which Discipline Topics to Focus On

Positive language and interactive modeling should top your list. Then think about other discipline topics that are most relevant to your school right now. For example, if your school has chosen to focus on recess or cafeteria discipline, discuss and practice with classroom teachers ways to teach their classes recess and lunch behavior, and discuss and practice with paraprofessionals effective ways to respond when children misbehave at recess or lunch.

Be sure to leave some flexibility for staff input as you plan topics. Adults, like children, generally learn best when they have opportunities to make their own choices and when they can connect their learning to their lives (Knowles, Holton, & Swanson, 2005). So give staff a say in topic and learning format, and make sure they get immediately useable skills and techniques from their trainings and discussions.

LEADING EFFECTIVE ADULT LEARNING

■ **Establish a climate of respect.** To wrestle together with a demanding topic such as discipline, staff need to have a climate of respect. One way to establish this climate during group discussions is to begin by establishing conversation norms. Ask the group, "If we want this conversation to be respectful and open, what specifically do we need to do?" Staff may answer, "Listen with an open mind," "Resist side conversations," and so forth. Record teachers' responses and post them as a reminder throughout the conversation.

■ **Offer some choice.** Give staff some say in what to learn about. Ask what discipline issues they want to work on (buddy teacher take-a-break? working with children with especially volatile tempers? something else?) and incorporate these into your agenda. Also give staff some choice in how they want to learn (for example, through all-staff discussions, a book study group, modeled lessons, or colleague observations).

■ **Provide practical solutions.** Be sure to provide and help staff practice strategies that they can use right away in their interactions with students. Look in the appropriate chapters of this book for concrete schoolwide discipline strategies to share with staff, depending on which issues they need help with. For classroom discipline strategies to share with classroom teachers, see *Rules in School: Teaching Discipline in the Responsive Classroom*, 2nd edition, 2011, available from www.responsiveclassroom.org.

- **Choose appropriate conversation formats.** Match the format to the goals of the conversation. For example, if the goal is to understand a discipline problem, it might work well to do an around-the-circle or partner sharing in which each person responds to a question you pose to the whole group. If the goal is to narrow down a list of possible solutions to a discipline problem, you might have each person name one idea she prefers and why, along with one idea she strongly opposes and why. Using an appropriate conversation format helps adults stay engaged and feel respected. (See Appendix C for more on conversation formats.)

- **Cultivate a habit of reflection.** In *The Adaptive School: A Sourcebook for Developing Collaborative Groups*, authors Garmston and Wellman write, "Any group too busy to reflect on its work is too busy to improve" (Garmston & Wellman, 2008, p. 155). When faced with a discipline problem, ask questions before diving into a solution. If lunchroom behavior isn't what it should be, ask the staff: What skills will students need if they're to have a pleasant lunch experience? How are we teaching and reinforcing those skills now? What further steps are needed? This reflection can reveal the true sources of the problem and lead to solutions that really work. (For a structure that teachers can use to reflect with colleagues about a student's behavior problem, see Appendix B.)

Delve Into the Details

To truly help staff handle the day-to-day behavior issues they face, trainings and discussions about discipline have to go into detail about what words and tone of voice to use when speaking to students, which exact routines need to be modeled, how exactly to escort a child to buddy teacher take-a-break, and so forth. Here are just a few ways you can ensure this kind of detailed learning:

- **Ask staff to share successes and challenges.** Lead them in sharing which discipline strategies worked or didn't work for them and why.

■ **Provide practice time.** During staff meetings, have adults practice discipline teaching techniques together and role-play how to handle discipline scenarios. Provide behavior scenarios for this practice or ask staff to name scenarios.

■ **Model being an engaged learner.** Join in on the questioning, practicing, and observing.

Structure Colleague Observations and Small-Group Conversations

School adults can gain a lot from one-on-one or small-group learning experiences around discipline. Here are two ideas for making this kind of learning happen at your school:

■ **Provide opportunities for staff to visit one another's classrooms.** This benefits both the observing and observed staff. The observing adult can get ideas from seeing a colleague in action, and the observed adult can benefit from honest and respectful feedback about her practice. Support these visits by providing coverage so that visiting teachers can leave their rooms, including covering a class yourself from time to time. Also be sure to allow time for teachers to reflect together after the visits. This reflection, even if it's only ten minutes, powerfully deepens learning.

■ **Consider establishing specialist meetings.** Art, music, PE, computer, and library teachers can provide important insights into discipline issues because they teach all students in the school and they see students in varied contexts. So in addition to including specialists when you set up classroom visits, think about structuring ways for specialists' insights to flow to other staff. For example, perhaps once a month the specialists can briefly meet as a group with the behavioral interventionist and one or two school leaders. This small group can talk about any children in the school who are having notable academic or social challenges and do any needed problem-solving.

Borrowing a Page From NPR

At Bywood Elementary in Upper Darby, Pennsylvania, principal Lisa Kostaneski knew she had to build trust and respect among staff if they were to have meaningful conversations about school discipline. To do this, she borrowed a page from National Public Radio. After hearing NPR's "This I Believe" essays, Kostaneski asked teachers to join her and other school leaders in writing informal statements about why they had gone into teaching and why they had stayed. Everyone would then bring these statements to a staff meeting.

Some of the teachers resisted at first, questioning why they needed to share their beliefs in writing. But as they began to write, many felt re-energized about teaching. They wrote stories about what they valued most about this profession, who inspired them along the way, and why they had chosen to remain in such a challenging job.

At the staff meeting, all the statements were pinned up on the walls, and the staff spent twenty minutes doing a gallery walk. Teachers said things to each other like "Pam, I didn't know your mom taught for thirty years in Philly" or "Stan, your high school coach really impacted your decision to teach!" Teachers not only learned what was important to their colleagues, but they drew inspiration from one another's stories.

In *The Courage to Teach*, Parker Palmer speaks about the value of encouraging teachers to explore this "inner landscape of teaching." He posits, "The more familiar we are with our inner terrain, the more surefooted our teaching—and living—become" (Palmer, 1999, p. 5). A corollary is that the more teachers understand their colleagues' inner teaching terrains, the deeper their mutual trust and respect become, and the more effective their collaboration on tough issues like discipline.

FINAL THOUGHT

Opening the Way to Lasting Change

When people have a positive learning experience, they tend to seek out more like it. This is true for children, and it's true for adults. A rich conversation with colleagues about a discipline strategy may lead a teacher to visit fellow teachers' rooms to see that strategy in action. A fruitful visit may lead two teachers to start a study group to delve deeper into the topic. The study group may lead to further refinement in teachers' practice. When teachers see the benefits of that refinement, they may be excited to share it with the entire school, which may lead to more rich conversations.

And so it goes, positive learning spawning more positive learning. When school leaders make adult learning and collaboration meaningful so that a critical mass of school staff willingly seek out better ways to teach discipline, an exciting momentum builds. That's when our schools are on their way to lasting change.

PART TWO

Positive Responses to Misbehavior

✦

Clear Response Procedures

SCHOOL LEADER'S CHECKLIST

❑ **Create a protocol for responding to misbehavior for all staff to follow**

   ❑ Address the misbehavior immediately with simple words, a signal, or moving closer to the child

   ❑ Use a nonpunitive consequence if needed

   ❑ Provide more intensive supports if needed

   ❑ Have the child leave the classroom or school for an extended period if needed

❑ **Establish a chain of support** (people that staff should call if they need help handling a behavior situation)

❑ **Establish a crisis response team** (for extreme situations that pose a threat to children's or adults' safety)

❑ **Help staff learn the protocol your school develops**

Provide it in writing:

   ❑ Staff handbook

   ❑ Quick cheat sheets

   ❑ Other: _____

❑ **Practice at staff meetings**

   ❑ Provide misbehavior scenarios for this practice

   ❑ Discuss how to use buddy teacher and private take-a-breaks

CHAPTER 9

Clear Response Procedures

Make sure all staff handle misbehavior consistently

The most powerful way to address students' misbehavior is to put strong, consistent effort into nurturing positive behavior in the first place. Establishing strong teacher-student relationships, creating rules with students, using positive language throughout the school, modeling and reinforcing skills and routines, frequently referring to the rules in guiding children's behavior day in and day out, designing engaging and appropriately challenging lessons, deliberately building a sense of community in the school—all these adult behaviors foster students' feelings of belonging, competence, and engagement, a prerequisite of positive student behavior.

Without these practices, our best efforts to handle misbehavior will fall short. With these practices, caring and safe student behavior will be the norm. But no matter how strong our foundation for discipline, children will sometimes misbehave. For those times, schools need to have clear procedures in place for all adults to follow in guiding the children back to positive behavior. This ensures that when a child makes a mistake, everyone remains safe, the child feels respected and learns from the mistake, and everyone gets back to productive learning as soon as possible.

To help you lead your school in creating and consistently using a set of procedures for responding to misbehavior, this chapter discusses:

- The goals in responding to misbehavior in the *Responsive School Discipline* approach

- A response protocol that achieves these goals

■ Establishing a clear chain of support and a crisis response team

■ Helping staff learn and practice the procedures your school develops

Goals in Responding to Children's Misbehavior

In the *Responsive School Discipline* approach, the goals in responding to children's misbehavior are to:

■ **Maintain safety and order.** A primary goal is to address the negative behavior and re-establish positive behavior as quickly and simply as possible so that the child can return to positive behavior, teachers can continue teaching, and all children can remain safe and learn productively.

■ **Help students recognize and fix their mistakes.** All children want to do well and can do well. Our responses to misbehavior, then, must give children opportunities to learn from their mistakes. We do this by giving children nonpunitive consequences, if needed, to help them see the effects of their actions and fix any damage.

■ **Help students develop internal control of their behavior.** Ultimately we want students not just to do as they're told, but to understand why expected behaviors are important and to develop the self-control to follow through. Our responses to misbehavior therefore must give children opportunities to talk with caring adults, if needed, about their mistakes and how to avoid similar mistakes in the future.

A Response Protocol That Achieves These Goals

The following protocol offers a range of nonpunitive responses for achieving the goals stated above:

1. Address the misbehavior with a simple response right when it starts.

2. Use a nonpunitive consequence if needed.

3. Provide more intensive supports if needed.

4. Have the child leave the classroom or school for an extended period if needed.

Each of these steps is explained in detail in the next few pages.

If your school adopts this or a similar protocol, make it clear to all staff that although generally it's best to begin with step 1 (the quickest and least interruptive response) and then proceed to further steps if needed, there are times when they should jump to a "later" step right away and times when they should skip steps. In making this judgment call, adults need to assess the type, frequency, and severity of the misbehavior, the safety risk to other children, which other adults are present and may be able to help, and other factors.

This protocol is therefore not meant to be followed in lockstep fashion, but to lay out the range of responses for school adults to take when a child is misbehaving. Regardless of which response is used, it's crucial to keep interventions respectful and always aim for helping the child return to positive behavior and productive learning.

1. Address the misbehavior with a simple response right when it starts

The most important thing to do about misbehavior is to address it right away. When children's behavior goes off track, they need to hear immediately from adults so they can break their momentum, change course, and move toward positive behavior. Although this may sound obvious, adults often let small misbehaviors go, not addressing them until they've escalated and are harder to reverse. So emphasize and re-emphasize to staff the importance of responding immediately. Help them learn these three simple ways:

- **Using reminding and redirecting language.** A few direct, respectful words can go a long way toward bringing children back to positive behavior. For example, Cynthia is trying to trip a classmate during a fire drill, thinking it's a funny joke. "Cynthia, what does our school-wide rule 'Be safe' need to look like during a fire drill?" her teacher says. (See Chapter 4 for more about reminding and redirecting language.)

- **Giving nonverbal signals.** A knowing glance, a subtle signal, or a gentle hand on the shoulder may be all that's needed to redirect a child toward positive behavior. For example, Ferdinand repeatedly bops the student one row ahead of him on the head with his cap. An adult puts a hand on Ferdinand's shoulder, and Ferdinand stops.

- **Moving closer to the child.** (Or having the child move closer to the adult.) These simple acts are other ways to help the child remember expected behavior. A lunch supervisor notices rude talking starting at a lunch table. She sits down at the table. Her presence gives the children the reminder they need, and the talking turns respectful.

2. Use a nonpunitive consequence if needed

Sometimes the above steps aren't enough. Perhaps a student needs more support to calm down from out-of-control behavior. Perhaps she needs help seeing the effect of her behavior and learning to be responsible for the consequences of her actions. In these situations, adults can use a nonpunitive consequence to help the child do the necessary learning.

Here are three basic types of nonpunitive consequences to choose from, depending on the situation. Help staff understand and gain facility in using them.

- **Simple reparation (also known as "you break it, you fix it").** When children can quickly and simply fix a mistake, having them do so often provides them the most effective learning. For example, "Roberta, use the paper towels to clean up the spill before joining our line." Fixing a mistake can also take the form of a simple "do over": "Rosaline, come here and try the condiments line again, considerately this time."

- **Increased structure and supervision.** In some instances of misbehavior, it's effective for adults to provide additional structures or bump up the level of supervision temporarily, perhaps for a class period, a day, or a few days. This might take the form of:

  - **Moving the child** away from where the misbehavior occurred (a child who distracts others at an all-school meeting is told to move to a different spot).

  - **Taking away objects** related to the misbehavior until adults are sure the child can handle the objects appropriately (a student who uses certain playground equipment dangerously must stop using it; the student talks with an adult about proper use and tries again in a day or two).

- **Narrowing a child's choices** ("Wanda, today during recess you'll need to choose the playground structure or the blacktop. You can try field games again tomorrow.").

- **Taking a privilege or responsibility away** from the child for awhile (a student messenger of the week who's disruptive in the halls loses that role for the rest of the week and needs to show that he can handle the responsibility before getting a turn at being messenger again).

■ **Take-a-break (a positive time-out).** To help children regain self-control, adults can respectfully have them take a short break in a designated place. While in take-a-break, the child sits quietly or uses calming techniques to regain self-control so he can come back and rejoin the group in a positive way. There are three types of take-a-break:

- **In-classroom take-a-break.** If the misbehavior takes place in a classroom, the teacher may have the student take a break at a designated spot in that room. The child rejoins the group when she has regained self-control. (This routine, like all forms of take-a-break, needs to be carefully taught to students before it's used. For details, see *Rules in School: Teaching Discipline in the Responsive Classroom*, 2nd edition, 2011, available from www.responsiveclassroom.org.)

- **Buddy teacher take-a-break.** If in-classroom take-a-break doesn't work, or if the teacher judges right away that the student needs to be away from the classroom or classmates to regain self-control, she may have the child take a break in a nearby buddy teacher's classroom. The child stays there until he's back in control and the teacher is ready to have him back in the classroom (usually by the end of a class period).

- **Private take-a-break.** If neither in-classroom nor buddy teacher take-a-break works, or if the teacher judges right away that the child needs to be away from any classroom or all students to regain self-control, the child may take a break in a private space in the school, such as a counselor's office, that's designated for this purpose. Like buddy teacher take-a-break, private take-a-break usually lasts until the end of a class period.

(See Chapter 10 for information about buddy teacher and private take-a-breaks.)

Keep in mind—and remind staff—that there is such a thing as a natural consequence. Often the most effective intervention is to allow a student to experience the consequence that naturally follows her behavior mistake rather than to impose a consequence, so long as that natural consequence isn't harmful or shameful to the child or other students. For example, if a child falls down when running in the hall, that child most likely has learned all she needs to learn. An adult who sees the running and the fall need not do anything except to express empathy: "That must've hurt!"

THREE Rs THAT MAKE CONSEQUENCES NONPUNITIVE

Help school adults understand, and continuously remind them, that what makes consequences nonpunitive are the "three Rs"—they're respectful, relevant, and realistic.

- **Respectful.** Instead of "Jimmy, I'm not going to put up with your antics today. You're annoying the other students," an adult might say "Jimmy, take a break from the game. I'll signal for you to come back in after awhile."

- **Relevant.** The consequence should be directly related to the misbehavior. If a child throws food in the cafeteria, a relevant consequence would be for the child to help clean up the mess, not, for example, to miss recess.

- **Realistic.** The consequence should be reasonable for the student and manageable for the adult. If a student writes on the bathroom wall, a realistic consequence would be for the student to clean that wall, not all the bathrooms in the building.

3. Provide more intensive supports if needed

In many cases, the above steps are enough to restore order and return the child to positive behavior. But sometimes children need more direct instruction or supervision to address a lack of skills or to build a repertoire of strategies for avoiding similar problems in the future. These additional follow-up supports may include:

- Teachers reteaching expected behaviors through interactive modeling, role-playing, practice, and reinforcing feedback.

- Teachers breaking down and simplifying procedures or increasing the degree of supervision and then slowly letting the child return to independence as he shows readiness for it.

- Teachers doing collaborative problem-solving through problem-solving conferences, class meetings, conflict resolution, or classroom behavior agreements (see *Solving Thorny Behavior Problems: How Teachers and Students Can Work Together* by Caltha Crowe, 2009, available from www.responsiveclassroom.org).

- A team of adults from school and home providing comprehensive interventions and crisis support for the child.

4. Have the child leave the classroom or school for an extended period if needed

In some situations, we may need to have children stay away from the classroom for longer than the usual buddy teacher or private take-a-break length of time. Or we may need them to stay away from school for one or more days. These extended breaks may be appropriate when a student is unable to return to positive behavior in a reasonable amount of time even with reasonable supports, when the behavior poses a significant safety risk to other children or adults, or when it's beyond a teacher's ability to manage the behavior. Options for these extended breaks include:

- **Keeping the student in private take-a-break longer than usual (in-school suspension).** A child could stay in private take-a-break for possibly the rest of the day. In this case, the teacher might send class work with the student, with the expectation that once she calms down and regains self-control, she will complete this work while away.

- **Sending the child home (at-home suspension).** If a student is physically out of control, your school will most likely need to give him an at-home suspension, notifying the parent to come pick up the child. Before the child rejoins the classroom, a school leader, the parent, teacher, and the child should meet to create a plan for supporting the student in returning to and sustaining positive behavior.

■ **Calling local security or emergency medical services.** This should be done only in extreme situations in which a child's behavior is beyond the school's ability to manage safely. If doing so will not further compromise safety, contact the students' parents before seeking outside medical or security assistance. Before the child returns to school, convene a team made up of a school leader, the parent, the child's teacher, the behavior interventionist, paraprofessionals who interact with the child, and other relevant school staff to create a comprehensive plan to support the child in re-entering school and staying on track.

Establish a Clear Chain of Support and a Crisis Response Team

School adults need to know that they're not alone when responding to students' misbehavior. Indeed, many of the actions in the above protocol require staff to involve other school adults.

Although classroom teachers, when they need help, will most often simply call on their buddy teacher and use the buddy teacher take-a-break strategy, they will need to call on a different adult if a student needs to go to private take-a-break (see Chapter 10 for details about these take-a-break strategies). Nonclassroom adults, as well, may need help from other staff in handling behavior incidents. And all school adults may need to call on a crisis response team member for extreme situations that pose a threat to children's or adults' safety.

Chain of support

For situations when adults need help from a colleague other than their buddy teacher (for example, to give a child a private take-a-break), it's important that school leaders establish a "chain of support," the sequence of designated go-to people and backup go-to people. Spelling out this information and clearly communicating it to all school adults means there will be less scrambling for support in the moment, more feelings of all adults being on a team, and greater safety and support for students.

Here's a sample written chain of support that would be passed out to staff. Whatever chain your school establishes, be sure to designate specific people for each step.

1. Call Ms. Davis, the school secretary, or send a student to Ms. Davis with a note or a "request for support" card. This alerts the office of the need for an immediate response.

2. Ms. Young, the principal, or Mr. Samuels, the assistant principal, will respond if possible.

3. If neither Ms. Young nor Mr. Samuels is available, Ms. Davis will call one of the following adults:

   a. Mr. Bedford, school counselor: Room _____, phone _____.

   b. Ms. Wiley, special education inclusion teacher: Room _____, phone _____.

   c. Ms. Felton, administrative intern: phone: _____.

   d. Ms. Vazquez, second grade teacher: Room _____, phone _____. (If Ms. Vazquez is needed, Ms. O'Brien next door will take Ms. Vazquez's class.)

Inform Parents

Once your school has established a chain of support and a crisis response team, tell parents about them. Spell out the steps and name the people involved. This specificity will reassure parents that if their children have a difficult day at school, there is a well-thought-out safety net there for them.

Crisis response team

In addition to the chain of support, establish a crisis response team for extreme situations in which children's or adults' safety is at risk. This team should be made up of several people who are trained in behavior de-escalation techniques and designated to drop everything in the event of an emergency and tend to the situation. (Find out your district's specific requirements for a crisis response team.)

Help Staff Learn and Practice the Procedures Your School Develops

After establishing a protocol for responding to misbehavior, a chain of support, and a crisis response team, be sure to communicate and frequently review the information with all staff. Don't assume that just because you have a written plan, everyone will implement it. Take time to build a shared understanding of what the plan will look and sound like in action, and provide plenty of opportunities for colleagues to practice with each other. Not only will this help all adults handle discipline situations consistently and effectively in the moment, but it will also build a stronger sense of community among the adults. Following are three actions you can take to make sure staff have the information and skills they need.

Provide handy written references

- **In the staff handbook:** Describe the response protocol, chain of support, and crisis response team in the staff handbook so staff can refer to this information at any time.

- **Quick cheat sheets:** Make cards that list the chain of support and instructions for activating help from the crisis team. Staff can then carry the cards with them, and teachers can put them in their plan books or near their classroom phones.

Use staff meetings to practice effective ways to address misbehavior

Join staff into pairs or small groups. Provide various misbehavior scenarios and have people practice using brief, firm, and respectful language or gestures to redirect children. Also have them practice deciding quickly on a nonpunitive consequence when necessary. Here are some scenarios to get you started. Ask staff for ideas of other effective ways to handle each scenario.

- Lola, a second grader, wants to join two other children in jumping rope at recess, but they won't let her, saying "No, this is private jump rope." (Possible responses: "Mattie and Emily, remember our 'Be kind' rule," "Girls, let others join in the way we practiced," or similar redirecting language.)

- At lunch, a student who finishes eating early gets up and wanders around, starting to bother the children at other tables. (Possible responses: Make eye contact with the student and point to the posted cafeteria procedures, which say to do the activities provided on the tables when you finish eating. Or say matter-of-factly to the student, "Luis, what should you be doing right now?")

- On the playground, Ernie, a fifth grader, is chasing a girl in his class who clearly doesn't want to be chased. (Possible response: Gently and calmly put a hand out as Ernie runs by and say in a firm, neutral voice, "Whoa, Ernie. Stay next to me for a minute." Then, when Ernie settles down, say, "OK, go play now, and remember to treat people the way they want to be treated.")

■ The class is walking in line toward the building exit at dismissal time. The first student in line turns around to walk backward so she can smile at her classmates. (Possible response: "Tamara, move to the end of the line. You can try being line leader again tomorrow.")

Model for teachers what to do if students need to leave the classroom

Chapter 10 offers a full explanation of the procedures for adults to follow when using buddy teacher and private take-a-breaks. For now, consider that practicing these strategies and learning how to activate the crisis response team are great uses of staff meeting time. Demonstrate (or ask a teacher leader to demonstrate) the following:

■ How to get help (including how to send a student to a buddy teacher to activate a buddy teacher take-a-break, and how to use the chain of support for a private take-a-break)

■ How to respond to requests for help (how to behave toward the student who needs to be escorted, including in situations when the child is clearly upset, out of control, or defiant)

■ How, as a classroom teacher, to welcome a child back into the room after a break

Interactive modeling, a technique for teaching routines and behaviors to children, can work well to demonstrate behaviors for adults as well. See "Sample Modeling for Staff: Getting Help From a Buddy Teacher" on page 145 in Chapter 10 for an example of how to use this technique with staff.

Also provide a demonstration of how to check in later in the day with a child who needed to take a break outside the classroom. This demonstration should show how to make sure the child understands why the behavior was a problem and how to identify some strategies for avoiding a similar problem in the future. (See page 144 in Chapter 10 for details.)

ENSURING EFFECTIVE RESPONSES TO MISBEHAVIOR

- **Help adults balance firmness with kindness.** Compare "Sally, how many times do I have to tell you to lower your voice? I've had it up to here!" with "Sally, take a break" (said in a calm and matter-of-fact manner when Sally starts to talk too loudly). The second way is both firm and kind, maintaining high expectations while preserving the child's dignity. Model and give staff chances to practice this kind of language. Emphasize the importance of addressing misbehaviors early—if we wait until we're frustrated, we're more likely to become sarcastic, blaming, or vengeful or to give up and not address the misbehavior at all.

- **Don't confuse consistency with one-size-fits-all.** Consistency means that all staff draw from the same set of positive responses and use the same firm, kind manner when handling misbehavior. It doesn't mean all staff should respond to every child in the same way. A student with an inflexible and explosive temperament may need a private take-a-break to avoid a meltdown. A student with attention struggles may need to work closer to the teacher to avoid a tantrum. Help staff develop the facility and confidence to respond to discipline problems based on their knowledge of the child and the nature of the behavior.

- **Instruct staff never to send an upset child out of the room or off the playground alone.** If staff send an anxious or frustrated child alone to a buddy teacher or tell an angry child to go alone from the playground to the school's private take-a-break place, the student may do something risky to himself or others along the way. Worse, the child may decide to leave school grounds. Impress upon staff that it's critically important they always use the established discipline protocol and chain of support to make sure children who need to leave their area for behavior reasons are continuously supervised.

- **Simplify paperwork.** For starters, eliminate laborious forms for initiating a buddy teacher or private take-a-break. Expecting teachers to complete lengthy requests for support could discourage them from seeking the appropriate backup. A lengthy request process also runs counter to our efforts to respond quickly and effectively to children's needs.

■ **Model an attitude of curiosity about what's motivating the behavior.** Help school adults see that often a misbehaving child is a child lacking essential skills or a child feeling insecure or rejected. Model thinking about what basic needs the child is attempting to meet through her behavior and how school adults can help her meet those needs in positive ways. (See "Being Thoughtful" below for more on responding in this way to children's misbehavior.)

■ **Model thinking about the child's strengths.** What skills, talents, and interests does the child currently have? How can school adults build on these strengths? Pose such questions when discussing individual children's behavior problems with staff. For example, if the student is a natural athlete, can the recess supervisor enlist her help in modeling safe recess soccer or basketball moves as a way to improve her recess behavior? Help school adults see that building on children's strengths leads to more effective solutions.

■ **Make it comfortable for staff to ask you for help.** School staff need to be comfortable asking school leaders for help with discipline issues before children's behavior problems get more serious or entrenched. Send a clear message that asking for help is a sign of being responsible, not a sign of weakness or incompetency. Then, whenever staff approach you, make sure your demeanor supports this message.

BABS REFLECTS

Being Thoughtful

When children misbehave, adults need to decide quickly how best to respond. The immediacy of the moment often doesn't afford us the time to think deeply about what the child may need. That's why having a well-understood and practiced protocol is so important.

But at a later time in the day, we do need to think about what may have contributed to the problem. What was the motivation behind the child's behavior? Is this student lacking a sense of belonging? Was this behavior a way to "research" which behaviors adults are really serious about? Does this child lack certain skills? Which skills? What are some of her interests, strengths, talents? Can we build on these positives in helping the child change her behavior?

We also need to think about our own behavior as the responsible adults in the child's school life. Have we sufficiently shown this student that we know her and appreciate her strengths? Have we made our expectations crystal clear? If we used a consequence for the misbehavior, was it respectful, relevant, and realistic? What further supports from adults might help? What needs to happen if we're to prevent similar issues in the future?

Without this thoughtfulness, we're merely reacting to misbehavior. As soon as we respond to one instance of misbehavior, another one pops up. Encouraging thoughtfulness among staff is a practical way to stop merely reacting and start truly teaching discipline.

FINAL THOUGHT

Assuming Positive Intentions

It's so important for school leaders to build a culture of assuming positive intentions behind children's misbehavior. If we adults hold firm to this assumption, especially when students' behaviors are the most challenging, our actions are more apt to communicate genuine respect and care for the child. When we understand that many of children's misbehaviors are persistent and fierce attempts to meet basic needs, we come to see misbehavior in a new way. Children do the best they can with the skills and resources they possess. When they falter, they need adults to teach them the skills they lack and provide the sense of safety and belonging they need. Our job, as school leaders, is to model giving this supportive response and to enable staff to do the same.

Positive Use of Time-Out

SCHOOL LEADER'S CHECKLIST

❏ **Establish a buddy teacher take-a-break system**

  ❏ Introduce the strategy to teachers

  ❏ Emphasize using the strategy nonpunitively

  ❏ Create pairs of buddy teachers

  ❏ Teach staff the steps in using the strategy

  ❏ Guide teachers on how to introduce the strategy to their class

  ❏ Remind teachers to use interactive modeling when introducing the strategy

❏ **Establish a private take-a-break system**
Follow all the relevant steps from above, plus:

  ❏ Designate a space and the personnel (chain of support; who stays with the child during the break; who walks the child back to the classroom afterward)

❏ **Communicate with parents about outside-the-classroom breaks**

  ❏ Explain the procedures in your beginning-of-year communications with parents

  ❏ Guide teachers on when and how to inform parents that their child needed an outside-the-classroom break

❏ **Familiarize staff with your district's requirements for handling extended breaks at school or home** (in-school and at-home suspensions)

Positive Use of Time-Out

Plan how to respectfully give children a break from the classroom when necessary

◆

I t's morning meeting time in Ms. Molan's fourth grade classroom. Jovita is sharing some news with her classmates. "Last week I got a new puppy from the shelter. He's black and brown and we named him Wally. He starts puppy class on Saturday. I'm ready for questions and comments."

Before any hands go up, Jeremiah leans over to Kevin and says under his breath, but loud enough for the class to hear, "I'll bet Wally fails puppy class." Ms. Molan responds calmly and quietly, "Jeremiah, take a break." Jeremiah protests loudly, "This isn't fair!" As he walks to the take-a-break spot, he stomps his feet and slaps a nearby desk.

Ms. Molan keeps her focus on the class, inviting questions for Jovita's sharing. "Why did you name him Wally?" a classmate asks. Meanwhile, over in the take-a-break spot, Jeremiah's behavior escalates. Ms. Molan slips a note to another student and says, "Matthew, please deliver this to Ms. Habib." As the sharing continues, Matthew quietly leaves the room.

Moments later, he returns with Ms. Habib. Ms. Molan says, "Jeremiah, go with Ms. Habib," and then redirects her attention to the group activity that the class is now engaged in. Jeremiah stomps to the door, and Ms. Habib escorts him to her room for a take-a-break there while Ms. Molan continues morning meeting with the class.

■ ■ ■

When children have behavior problems in their classroom, teachers can respond with a range of strategies, from giving a respectful reminder or redirection, to providing increased supervision, to having the student go to the take-a-break (or positive time-out) spot for awhile to regroup. But as the above story shows, there are times when the behavior is disruptive enough or escalates enough that the child needs to take a break from the classroom so that he can cool down and the other children can keep learning.

For these times, it's important that school leaders set up a system to ensure that the breaks are handled in a safe, respectful, and supportive way for all involved—children and adults. One such system involves establishing buddy teacher take-a-break and private take-a-break. Both of these are ways to give children positive time-outs in a safe, supervised spot other than their classroom. This is helpful because leaving the classroom scene for awhile can sometimes be just the thing to help upset children pull themselves back together.

Both buddy teacher and private take-a-breaks require school adults to work together so that at all times, they form a coordinated safety net for children who are upset and need adult support to regain composure and return to productive learning. This chapter discusses these two take-a-break options and the key steps that you, as a school leader, can take to ensure that staff work as a team to implement them well.

Buddy Teacher Take-a-Break

The opening story of this chapter shows the use of buddy teacher take-a-break. In this strategy, a classroom teacher calls for a colleague—a buddy teacher—to come and matter-of-factly escort a misbehaving student to her classroom. The student takes a break in a distraction-free spot there, with the buddy teacher keeping an eye on him to keep him safe. After awhile, when the student has had sufficient time to pull himself together, his classroom teacher comes to take him back to their room and warmly welcomes him back into the classroom activity.

When to use this strategy

Often it makes sense for teachers to try buddy teacher take-a-break after an in-room take-a-break proves ineffective. Other times, depending on the severity of the child's upset and other factors, it's appropriate to move the student out of the room immediately, before trying an in-room break. For example, if a teacher knows from experience that a student will become more upset if told to take an in-room break, or that certain classroom dynamics will prevent an in-room break from working well for this student, it may be beneficial to try the buddy teacher option immediately.

Benefits of this strategy

Three important benefits of buddy teacher take-a-break are that it:

- **Gives the child *and* teacher space.** Children are often better able to collect themselves when they're away from their classmates and their triggers for misbehavior. Teachers, too, often benefit from having some space from the student. After finding a calm Jeremiah in Ms. Habib's room, for example, Ms. Molan brings him back to their room, saying in a warm, friendly way, "We're working on the personal narratives that we started yesterday. After you get your folder, I'll meet you at your desk to help you get started." Ms. Molan's manner may not have been so positive if she hadn't had the space away from him to collect herself.

- **Keeps the teaching momentum going.** When a misbehaving child can gain the teacher's attention and energy, the unintended result may be that the misbehavior escalates and the whole class loses precious learning time. Using a buddy teacher take-a-break allows the teacher to keep her focus and energy on the class's learning. For example, had Jeremiah not left the room, he might have derailed Ms. Molan's attention from that day's morning meeting and disrupted her ability to maintain the tone of the classroom.

- **Prevents power struggles.** Having a colleague come take the student away for awhile stops the situation from escalating and effectively prevents a power struggle. When teachers prevent a power struggle, they preserve their relationship with the child, which is so essential to the child's positive learning.

Establishing a Buddy Teacher Take-a-Break System

Here are the key leadership steps in this work:

- Introduce buddy teacher take-a-break to teachers.

- Emphasize the importance of using this strategy nonpunitively.

- Create pairs of buddy teachers.

- Teach staff the steps of buddy teacher take-a-break.

- Guide teachers on how to introduce this strategy to their class.

- Remind teachers to model buddy teacher take-a-break behaviors.

Introduce buddy teacher take-a-break to teachers

At a staff meeting or a professional development training, introduce (or have a teacher leader introduce) buddy teacher take-a-break as an addition to teachers' repertoire of positive responses to children's misbehavior. Share with them the information above on when to use buddy teacher take-a-break and the benefits of this strategy.

You can also provide staff with readings about this strategy (for example, "Buddy Teachers: Lending a Hand to Keep Time-Out Positive and Productive," by Ruth Sidney Charney and Alice Yang, available at www. responsiveclassroom.org).

Emphasize the importance of using this strategy nonpunitively

The take-a-break strategy will work only if it's used nonpunitively. Help staff see that if we want students to return to positive behavior and productive learning, we must use words, body language, and a tone of voice that show we're not punishing them when we tell them to take a break. The fact that most children are used to thinking of being sent out of the classroom as a punishment makes it even more important that adults use a calm, neutral demeanor.

Acknowledge to staff that this can sometimes be an uphill battle. In the moment of a child's misbehavior, it's easy for a frustrated adult to use take-a-break with anger. Show understanding and encourage staff to strive hard to project calmness and evenness, even if they don't *feel* calm or even. Your encouragement makes a big difference.

KEEPING OUT-OF-CLASSROOM BREAKS NONPUNITIVE

■ **Frequently remind staff of the goals.** Remind staff that the goal of buddy teacher and private take-a-break is to help children regain self-control by giving them a space away from their classmates and classroom. Make sure they understand that these strategies are not intended to be a way for teachers to relinquish responsibility for a child. The teacher is responsible for knowing how the student did during the break and helping the child ease back into classroom activity afterward.

■ **Support strong teacher-student relationships.** As with all positive discipline practices, the success of buddy teacher and private take-a-break depends on a strong teacher-student relationship forged before the need to use the strategy. This relationship helps children trust that their teacher always has their best interests at heart, including when their teacher has them leave the room for a break. An important job of school leaders is to build a school culture in which teachers deliberately cultivate positive relationships with students.

■ **Help teachers practice a matter-of-fact tone.** Both the sending teacher and the escorting teacher should keep their talking firm, calm, and to a minimum. Spend time in staff meetings practicing this way of interacting with a child. Remind staff that the moment of misbehavior is not the time for lengthy conversations. Discussions about the problem behavior are best saved for later, when the child is calm and able to reflect.

■ **Emphasize the "welcome back" step.** Make sure teachers see it as an integral step, not an afterthought, to welcome a child back from buddy teacher take-a-break. When teachers warmly say something like "Stella, it's good to have you back. We're starting partner reading. Go get your book and join Jack. He's waiting for you," they provide the child with a clean slate. This kind of welcome, audible and visible to the rest of the class, affects not only how the child views herself, but also how classmates view her.

Create pairs of buddy teachers

Have teachers pair up for the year for the purposes of buddy teacher take-a-break. Guide teachers in considering these issues when pairing up:

- **The grades they teach.** Teachers of older children may want to partner with colleagues who teach a different grade, since older children may be embarrassed to be seen by students they know when they're in buddy teacher take-a-break. In the younger grades, it's usually fine for same-grade teachers to be buddies.

- **How free they are to leave their rooms.** If your district has a policy against teachers leaving their classrooms, or if teachers are simply uncomfortable leaving their rooms for even a few minutes to go to a buddy's room to escort a child to or from buddy teach take-a-break, they'll want to buddy with next-door or across-the-hall colleagues. That way, they'll be able to stand at their classroom door to receive or send the student while keeping an eye on their own class.

- **For special area teachers, whether they need an administrator's support.** Special area teachers can and should be part of this system, but they'll need to consider how distant their rooms are from other classrooms. For example, Ms. Park, the art teacher, can have Mr. Grant, a regular classroom teacher, as a buddy. But if the art room is far from Mr. Grant's room, Ms. Park may need to have an administrator or another designated adult step in to walk a child from her room to Mr. Grant's so that Mr. Grant isn't pulled away from his room for too long. In this setup, at the end of the period Ms. Park would come to Mr. Grant's room to escort the child back to the child's regular classroom.

- **The need for a backup plan.** There will be occasions when a buddy isn't in her classroom when she's needed. Teacher pairs therefore need to identify one or two backup adults ahead of time. A learning specialist, special area teacher, or librarian might be able to serve in this role.

Teach staff the steps of buddy teacher take-a-break

Make sure all staff are clear on the following steps so that the whole school uses this procedure consistently. Use staff or grade-level meeting time to talk about this procedure and allow teachers to practice effective words and body language for each step. A great way to do this is to use interactive modeling. This technique for teaching routines and behaviors to children (see Chapter 5) is effective with adults as well. See "Sample Modeling for Staff: Getting Help From a Buddy Teacher" on page 145 for an example of how to use this technique.

■ **The teacher sends for the buddy teacher's help.** Often this is done by sending another student to deliver a note or a verbal message (for example, "Ms. Boswell needs you to come to our room").

Impress upon staff that the teacher requesting help should not go to the buddy teacher herself because doing so means leaving the distressed child unsupervised. It can also signal that misbehaving is a way to pull the teacher's attention away from the class.

■ **The buddy teacher arrives and escorts the child.** Stress how critically important it is that adults never have the child go alone to the buddy teacher's room. An upset, out-of-control child might not make it to the intended destination or might harm himself, others, or school property. He may even decide to leave the building.

When escorting the child, the buddy teacher should not converse or engage with the child, but simply be present to keep him safe. The classroom teacher continues to teach and work with the class while the student is being picked up.

■ **After a short while, the teacher picks up the child from the buddy room.** Make sure staff know that a buddy teacher take-a-break should be short, just long enough for the student to settle down and be ready to re-engage positively with classroom activity, and just long enough for the teacher to be ready to welcome the child back.

When the classroom teacher judges it's time for the child to return, she goes to the buddy teacher room to check in with the child. If the child is calm and ready to rejoin the class, the teacher escorts the child back to the classroom. It's important that the teacher clearly and earnestly welcomes the child ("Ben, I'm glad to bring you back to our room. We're doing our science observations. Your group is eager to have you join them."). Emphasize to staff that the goal is to communicate faith in the child's ability to re-engage with learning.

■ **Later in the day, the teacher has a longer check-in with the student if needed.** The purpose of this check-in is to make sure the child understands why she needed the break and to brainstorm possible strategies to prevent a similar problem in the future. Clarify for staff that it's the classroom teacher's job, not the buddy teacher's, to do this check-in because the classroom teacher has the closest relationship with the child. Another reason is that the child is unlikely to be in a frame of mind to hold such conversations while still in the buddy teacher's room.

Let teachers know that in general, these are the key points to focus on in this check-in:

♦ **The child's positive standing with the teacher and the class.** ("I'm glad to have you back learning with us, Jeremiah. I noticed that when you came back from Ms. Habib's room you remembered our rules for writing time and got right to work on your story and worked quietly.")

♦ **What happened and why the take-a-break was needed.** ("Why do you think I sent you to Ms. Habib's room? What did you do when you were in take-a-break in our room?")

♦ **What the child can do differently next time.** ("What can you do next time you're taking a break in our room and you're mad? Would you like to know some things that other people, including myself, do when we're mad but we're not in a place where we can stomp and shout?" The teacher can then teach Jeremiah strategies such as tightening and relaxing hands and feet, squeezing a small ball, and deep breathing.)

Remind teachers that for persistent problems, they may need to engage the child in an additional problem-solving conference or use other collaborative problem-solving techniques (see *Solving Thorny Behavior Problems: How Teachers and Students Can Work Together* by Caltha Crowe, 2009, available from www.responsiveclassroom.org).

Sample Modeling for Staff: Getting Help From a Buddy Teacher

Step	*What you might say and do*
1. Describe the action you will model.	"When you need a student to take a break in a buddy teacher's room, the first step is to let your buddy teacher know that you need help while staying calm and keeping your attention on the class. Watch while I demonstrate how to do that."
2. Model the action.	Designate one staff member as a student messenger. Write a quick note on a piece of paper, walk over to the messenger, and whisper, "Pedro, take this note to Ms. Dennis." Immediately return your attention to the "class" while keeping an eye on the misbehaving student but not interacting with her.
3. Ask staff what they noticed.	"What did you notice about how I did that?" (If necessary, prompt with questions such as "What did you notice about my tone of voice and body language?" and "What did I do after I sent the messenger off?")
4. Ask a staff volunteer to model the action.*	"Anybody else want to demonstrate letting your buddy teacher know you need help?"
5. Ask the group what they noticed.*	"What did you notice about _____'s demonstration?"
6. Have the group practice.	Have staff form small groups. Group members take turns being the teacher requesting help while other group members observe and give feedback. Walk around to watch and listen.
7. Provide feedback.	"I heard a lot of matter-of-fact, succinct language and saw a lot of neutral body language. I saw people staying calm and staying focused on what they were doing with the class. That's an effective way to handle buddy teacher take-a-break."

*OK to skip steps 4 and 5.

Guide teachers on how to introduce this strategy to their class

Point out that buddy teacher take-a-break is not something to introduce during the first few weeks of school. It should be saved until after classroom rules and basic routines have been taught and in-classroom take-a-break is up and running.

When it's time to introduce buddy teacher take-a-break to the class, teachers should cover the following key points. Go over these points with staff and share with them the sample language provided:

- **The purpose of buddy teacher take-a-break.** "In our classroom," a teacher can say, "there may be times when it's hard to follow the rules or when you may need help with your self-control. We've all been practicing some strategies for regaining control in take-a-break in our classroom. But sometimes that might not be enough to help you settle down. Sometimes just being in the classroom makes it hard for you to settle down. One way that the teachers in this school are going to help you at times like that is by having you take a break in another classroom. We're going to call that a 'buddy teacher take-a-break.' The purpose is to help you regain control if you're not able to do it in this classroom."

- **Who the buddy teacher is and how the procedure will work.** "Ms. Williams and I are buddy teachers this year," a teacher might say. "That means you may need to go to her room to take a break sometimes, and students from Ms. Williams' class may occasionally need to take a break in our room. If I think you need to take a break in Ms. Williams' room, she'll come to our door to get you. When it's time for you to come back to our room, I'll go to her room to walk back to our room with you."

- **What's expected of students when they're in buddy teacher take-a-break.** "We have the same expectations for buddy teacher take-a-break as we do for our classroom take-a-break," a teacher might explain. "The take-a-break area in Ms. Williams' room is next to their classroom library. There's a chair and a small basket of books nearby. We'll be visiting her room later this morning so you can see the space. When you're in Ms. Williams' room, your job will be to make yourself calm so that you can come back to this classroom ready to cooperate and learn. You can sit quietly or look at one of the books, or sometimes I may ask you to take your class work with you to complete there after you've settled down."

Remind teachers to model buddy teacher take-a-break behaviors

Students need to see new routines modeled if they're to be successful at them, and the buddy teacher routine is no different. Remind teachers to use interactive modeling (see Chapter 5) to teach and guide students in practicing this routine. The modeling should cover these specifics:

- Walking quietly and calmly out of the classroom with an adult

- Calming down in the buddy teacher's room

- Re-entering the classroom after a buddy teacher take-a-break

- As classmates in the sending and receiving rooms: Keeping eyes, ears, and bodies focused on the learning activity and not on the student who is going to buddy teacher take-a-break

- As classmates in the sending room: Showing respect to the returning student and offering help if the student has a question about what the class is doing

Obviously, the usual "whole-class practice" step of interactive modeling won't work for buddy teacher take-a-break because the whole class can't practice this procedure at once, and having students practice one by one would take too long. Suggest to teachers that they might consider instead taking the whole class over to the buddy teacher's room to become familiar with the take-a-break location there.

Private Take-a-Break

Sometimes teachers, even the most skillful ones, find both in-classroom responses and a buddy teacher take-a-break insufficient for handling children's misbehavior. Perhaps the child refuses to go with the buddy teacher, or the behavior continues to escalate while the child is in the buddy classroom. Perhaps a student repeats a disruptive behavior after returning from the buddy room. At times students throw things, lash out violently, or have other behavior right from the start that's beyond the teacher's ability to redirect. Such behavior makes it unsafe to keep the student around peers for either in-classroom or buddy classroom intervention.

In all these cases, we need to give teachers a fall-back strategy. A strategy that often works is to have students take a break in a private space in the school, such as a counselor's office, a portion of the behavior interventionist's office, or some other space with an adult present to keep them safe.

When the student has regained self-control and her classroom teacher is ready to welcome her back, the classroom teacher or a designated adult comes to the break space to walk the child back to the classroom. As with buddy teacher take-a-break, children usually need to stay in private take-a-break for a fairly short amount of time, perhaps for the rest of a class period, although occasionally a longer break is needed (see "Extended Breaks" on page 150).

Called by a variety of names (for example, Student Resource Room, Back-on-Track Room, Rest and Recovery Room, and Safe Landing Room), this calm, private, supervised recovery space is a safety net for students—and teachers.

Benefits of private take-a-break

Like buddy teacher take-a-break, a private take-a-break allows the teaching momentum to continue, gives both the teacher and student space for calming down, and helps prevent power struggles. In addition, it:

- **Removes the child's audience.** This is important because for some children, calming down and regaining self-control within view of classmates or schoolmates is virtually impossible.

- **Affords the child more dignity than the traditional office visit.** Traditionally, children sent to the office for misbehavior are told to sit in the reception area until the principal or assistant principal is ready to see them. There they must endure the puzzled or knowing looks of everyone who passes through the office—students, parents, teachers, even visitors. A break in the counselor's office or another private space removes this extra layer of embarrassment and stress so that students can better regain their composure and retain their dignity.

Establishing a Private Take-a-Break System

The steps in creating a private take-a-break system mirror those of buddy teacher take-a-break. But you'll need to take the following additional steps:

Designate a space

Your school may or may not have unused classrooms or offices that can be turned into a private take-a-break space. If you don't have such spaces, consider using part of an existing room or a quiet area of the library. Whatever the space, it should be:

- **Private, away from high traffic areas.** Children who are already exhibiting extreme behaviors can get more extreme if they're on public display. They can also get too much attention for their negative behavior and become identified as "the troublemaker."

- **Soothing and distraction free.** An environment with too much stimulation or commotion may contribute to children's frustration or anxiety and make it difficult for them to regain self-control.

- **Student-friendly.** Whether students are spending a few minutes in private take-a-break or staying half a day or longer, the space needs to accommodate a child's physical needs. Comfortable student-sized chairs and desks, a table, and books, paper, pencils, and other basic materials contribute to a welcoming environment. They also allow students who need an extended break to do class work while they're away from their classroom.

Designate the personnel

As discussed in Chapter 9, you'll need to establish a chain of support that names whom staff should call if they need to have a child go to private take-a-break and who will go to a classroom to escort the child to the break space. In addition, name who will stay with the student during this recovery time and who will walk the child back to the classroom afterward. Administrators, counselors, social workers, and interventionists are the most common personnel for these roles.

Whomever your school chooses, it's critical that these individuals drop

Extended Breaks

Like a buddy teacher take-a-break, a private take-a-break should last only as long as needed for the child to regain self-control and the teacher to be ready to welcome the child back. In most cases, this means a break for the rest of a class period.

But sometimes a student's behavior is so disruptive that she needs to be out of the classroom for half a day or the rest of the day (in-school suspension) or needs to take a break at home (at-home suspension). Be sure to familiarize staff with your district's specific requirements for handling these extended breaks.

Here are two additional suggestions:

✦ **For extended breaks at school:** Consider having teachers send class work with the child to complete in the private break space after she calms down. This shows the child that she's responsible for learning, regardless of whether she's in the classroom or not.

✦ **For extended breaks at home:** Hold a re-entry meeting attended by the student, the parent, the teacher, and an administrator. Make a plan for how the school and home will support the child in maintaining positive behavior.

everything to attend to a child needing a private break. So plan backup people in case the designated adults are unavailable.

Be sure all staff are familiar with these role designations ahead of time so that they can use the system quickly and smoothly when a situation comes up. Put this information in your staff handbook and review it from time to time at staff meetings. You may also want to provide quick cheat sheets that staff can post in convenient spots.

Communicating With Parents About Outside-the-Classroom Breaks

It's important that parents understand your school's use of buddy teacher and private take-a-break. In your communications with them about discipline early in the year, explain these strategies, their purposes, and the particulars of your school's procedures for their use.

Emphasize the nonpunitive nature of these strategies. Some parents may feel that if their child needed a break for behavior reasons at school, they should piggyback some punishment at home. If you stress the school's positive use of these breaks, parents may assume an attitude that is more consistent with the school's. You can also encourage teachers to send reminder explanations home from time to time.

Also guide teachers on when and how to inform parents when their child needed a break outside the classroom. Teachers will need to know:

■ **Which situations they need to report.** Schools vary on this question. Assess your school's culture in deciding on a policy. Consider, at a minimum, requiring teachers to always inform parents in the case of a private take-a-break.

■ **How to inform parents.** Suggest to staff that a quick phone call or note is usually sufficient for letting parents know of their child's outside-the-classroom break. Emphasize the importance of using a direct and unbiased tone that conveys confidence in the child's ability to fix the mistake (see sample note on this page). If the situation warrants, more involved communications with parents can follow (see Chapter 11 for more on working with parents to solve behavior problems).

When a Student Had an Outside-the-Classroom Break

Sample Note to Parents

Dear _____,

I wanted to let you know that Jeremiah has been working hard during writer's workshop to add details to his writing and to follow our class rules of working quietly during that time.

I also wanted to let you know that this morning Jeremiah needed to take a break in Ms. Habib's class. (At Back to School Night, I explained that there are times when children may need a short break outside of our classroom so they can regain self-control.)

During morning meeting today, Jeremiah had to take a break in our room because he was saying negative things about a classmate's puppy when she was sharing about it. Jeremiah got mad about having to take a break and started shouting and stomping. He then took a break in Ms. Habib's room, and about ten minutes later he was back in charge of himself. When I had him rejoin our class, he came in quietly and followed our writing workshop procedures.

Jeremiah and I later talked about ways people help themselves calm down when they're mad. You might want to ask him which idea he picked to try next time he's feeling angry. We will also continue to practice at school, and I know Jeremiah will be successful.

Thank you for your continued support.

Sincerely,

[Teacher's name]

Throwing Out a Lifeline

Although many teachers crave adult collaboration, they sometimes resist using buddy teacher or private take-a-break. Too often, teachers are concerned that needing help from a colleague will reflect poorly on them. They worry that school leaders will see it as a sign of failure, of poor classroom management.

Nothing could be further from the truth, and it's impossible to over-assure teachers of this. I've learned how critical it is for leaders to send a strong message to staff that they view the use of buddy teacher and private take-a-break as good teaching practice. It makes a huge difference when a principal introduces these strategies during a staff meeting and has teachers role-play using them. It makes a huge difference when school leaders facilitate staff conversations about the rationale behind these strategies and continuously signal that teachers have permission to use them if needed.

Teachers need to know that when they're facing persistent or escalating behavior problems, they have a network of support within the school. They need to see that teaching does not have to be a private enterprise. They need to be assured of their school leaders' belief that working together sometimes means throwing out a lifeline to a colleague.

FINAL THOUGHT

Who Among Us?

Who among us, adults and children, hasn't needed a moment to regroup after a mistake? Who among us hasn't needed some space to reflect on our actions and create a plan for re-engaging positively with others? By removing the shame and humiliation from these moments for children, we can keep school a nurturing place for them, even during rocky times, and allow them to experience the greatest learning.

CHAPTER 11

Conferencing With Parents When There's a Problem

❑ **Encourage teachers to give parents a quick FYI about small incidents**

❑ **Provide teachers with ongoing training in communicating with parents about problems**

❑ **Teach teachers what to do if a conference gets tense**

❑ **If a conference is needed, be involved from the start**

    ❑ Discuss with the teacher whether you should come

❑ **Guide teachers on how to prepare for a conference**

    ❑ Provide a checklist of prep steps

❑ **Remind teachers to follow up after a conference**

Conferencing With Parents When There's a Problem

Take a team approach to helping the child

Haim Ginott, in his seminal work *Teacher and Child*, says that one of the cardinal rules of communication is to "talk to the situation, not the personality or character" (Ginott, 1972, p. 84). Ginott was talking about teachers communicating with students, but his rule also applies perfectly to school adults communicating with parents. In fact, it's probably the most important rule to keep in mind when we talk with parents about their child's behavior.

Most likely this communication will involve a problem-solving conference—a face-to-face conversation in which the parent and one or more school adults discuss challenges the child is facing and together identify strategies to help the child improve. Teachers will usually be the ones holding these conferences, but school leaders play the key role of providing guidance. School leaders may also come to the conferences themselves, especially in the case of persistent or unusually serious discipline problems.

If teachers and school leaders have done enough positive communication with parents all along (see Chapter 7), there will be a level of trust between home and school, and the collaborative problem-solving will be easier.

But even under the most positive of conditions, talking with parents about their child's struggles can be challenging. It's understandable for us on the school side to feel somewhat uneasy when we have to communicate information that may be difficult for parents to hear. Will the information be well received? Will our body language and words convey the intended message? Will we be able to engage the parent in meaningful dialogue?

Parents, for their part, sometimes react defensively, which is also understandable, since it's parents' job to advocate for the needs and rights of their children. Under these circumstances, it's easy for the conversation to deteriorate and leave both sides feeling personally attacked, the child's best interests all but forgotten.

To avoid this outcome, school leaders should, as part of the ongoing professional development of teachers, help them acquire skills in communicating with parents about children's behavior problems, and then, when the need for a conference comes up, be ready to offer needed supports. This important work will help ensure that problem-solving conferences with parents are respectful and, as Ginott suggests, focused on the situation: what's challenging the child and how to help her successfully deal with the challenge.

This chapter discusses these key steps for school leaders:

- Encourage teachers to give parents a quick FYI about small incidents.

- Provide ongoing training in communicating with parents about problems.

- If a conference is needed, be involved from the start.

- Don't delay a needed conference.

- Guide teachers on how to prepare for a conference.

- Remind teachers to follow up after a conference.

Encourage Teachers to Give Parents a Quick FYI About Small Incidents

There's benefit in teachers letting parents know of small behavior incidents before they become big problems, even if the issue was resolved. The small incidents may never become big, but if they do, these "just FYI" communications will have prepared parents if, later, a problem-solving conference or other problem-solving step is needed. And simply being prepared can go a long way toward smooth problem-solving.

Share with teachers the following to-do's in these early communications with parents:

- **Call or send a short note.** When the goal is to inform, not to problem-solve, a brief communication is usually all it takes. "Anjali had a bit of a challenging time at lunch today," a teacher might write in a note. "She created a ball out of her foil and threw it across the room. After taking a break to calm down, she was fine for the rest of lunch. She collected herself and the rest of the day was smooth."

- **Use a respectful, matter-of-fact tone.** As in the note about Anjali, teachers should describe factually and in a positive tone what the problem was and how they responded. This can show parents that the school is attentive to making sure their child is always conducting herself as a positive school member and reassure them that their child is emotionally safe at school. Suggest that if teachers write a note, they have a colleague or administrator read it for clarity, tone, and appropriateness before they send it. You can even devote some time to practicing note writing at a staff meeting.

One simple but very helpful step you can take is to let parents know, in your beginning-of-year general communications about school discipline, that their child's teacher may from time to time inform them of small behavior issues their child had. Make it clear that the school's intention behind these notes or phone calls is generally just to inform and not necessarily to ask the parent to take any action. This can help parents receive the information in the "just FYI" spirit intended and refrain from over-worrying or from punishing the child.

Provide Ongoing Training in Communicating With Parents About Problems

Being proactive—helping staff develop skills in conducting a potentially difficult conversation *before* they need to have one—is so critical to the conversation's going well. Use staff meeting time to help staff understand and practice the following important skills. (You can also lead book studies about communicating with parents. Two possible books to study are *Parents and Teachers Working Together* by Carol Davis and Alice Yang, 2005, available from www.responsiveclassroom.org, and *The Essential Conversation: What Parents and Teachers Can Learn from Each Other* by Sara Lawrence-Lightfoot, 2003.)

Warmly inviting a parent into a conversation

In contacting parents to ask for a conference and in welcoming them when they arrive and sit down at the conference, it's important that teachers use a warm tone and express a desire to work together.

For example, in extending the invitation, a teacher might say, "Ms. Engle, this is Maurice's teacher calling. We've noticed that Maurice is having some trouble at recess lately. I'd like to set up a conference for us to talk about strategies for helping him have a more positive recess experience." And in welcoming the parent at the conference, she might say, "Thank you for coming in today to talk about how we can best support Maurice. I'll be sharing some of the strategies we've been using at school, and I'm equally interested in hearing your ideas." Help staff practice this kind of language.

Starting a conference by naming the child's positives

Before launching into the problem, the teacher should name some of the child's strengths or interests. For example, "Maurice shows great passion for games. It's obvious that he enjoys figuring out strategies, and he comes up with some very creative ones." This shows parents that the school knows and appreciates their child.

Of course, naming strengths or interests requires teachers to observe for positives in the child, not just problems. Create a culture, through reminders and your own example, in which school adults do this—not only in preparation for a problem-solving conference with parents, but always.

Describing the problem and goal in a nonjudgmental way

Have teachers practice describing a child's problematic behavior in a factual, objective way. This helps keep the conversation focused on the behavior and not the child's character or personality. For example, "Neil has been teasing some of the younger students on the bus. He calls them names and says he'll hurt them if they tell a teacher. Today three students reported that they don't feel safe when Neil is on the bus."

It's also important to have teachers practice stating the goal for the child in a nonjudgmental way: "Our goal is to help Neil follow the bus rules and be respectful of others, especially the younger students." Note that the goal is stated positively—what the child should do rather than what he should not do.

> **Putting It All Together Through Role-Playing**
>
> Role-playing teacher–parent problem-solving conferences is a good way to help teachers pull together all the communication skills they're learning. At a staff meeting, provide a conference scenario. (For example, Emma has been scaring the other children with physical aggression and mean language during recess. The problem has reached a point where a conference with Emma's dad is needed.)
>
> Conduct a fishbowl style role-play, in which a few adults act out this conversation, one of them playing the role of the teacher and the others playing the role of parents and other family members who also came to the conference. The other staff at the meeting watch. After the role-play, these observers name the effective words, body language, listening, and so forth, that they heard and saw.
>
> Alternatively, you can pair staff up to do partner role-plays and then have everyone reflect on the experience afterward as a whole group.

Conveying faith in the child

Parents need to hear that the school is confident that their child can do well. For example, "We want Neil to be able to ride the bus without these incidents. It's going to take some practice and self-control for Neil to change this behavior, but we know he can do it." Listen for this kind of affirmation as teachers practice conference communication skills, and reinforce it.

Describing supports given to the child so far

Explain to teachers the importance of assuring parents that the school has been supporting the child in improving his behavior. Guide them to simply and factually describe this support. For example, a teacher might say, "Mr. Mellon, the bus driver, has moved Neil to the front of the bus. When Neil gets onto the bus, Mr. Mellon makes a point of greeting him in a friendly way and reminding him of the rules. When the bus arrives at school, Neil checks in with me to talk a bit about how the ride went."

Using a united "we" voice

Frequently remind teachers to use a "we" voice that invites cooperation throughout the conference. For example:

- "I know we're going to be able to help Neil with . . ."

- "By giving consistent messages at home and school, we can work together to help Neil . . ."

- "How might we work together to solve this problem?"

Asking open-ended questions to learn from the parents

Teachers can learn a lot about the child and about the parent's point of view by asking open-ended questions. What they hear in response can be invaluable in helping them understand the problem more clearly and collaborating more effectively with parents on solutions. Some examples of effective open-ended questions for this purpose are:

- "Can you tell me more about Mia's experience with that?"

- "What has helped Emily in the past with that challenge?"

- "What are some strategies that have helped Brian?"

- "What might I need to know about Lila that would help me better support her at school?"

- "What are you noticing at home?"

- "What has Orlando shared about what's happening at school?"

You can lead a brief exercise in which teachers practice crafting similar open-ended questions. Ask them to think of behavior scenarios they've recently encountered among their students and to come up with some open-ended questions they could ask a parent if they were conferencing about that issue.

Suspending judgment or inner dialogue when parents are speaking

It's so important that teachers genuinely listen when parents are talking, rather than working out their own ideas or thinking about how they'll respond. Emphasize to teachers that productive, respectful two-way conversations can occur only when school adults listen hard for parents' needs, fears, and deepest aspirations for their children.

Paying attention to body language

Advise teachers that leaning in slightly with arms uncrossed conveys interest and respect. Let them know that it's also important to maintain eye contact (or show other signals of attention and respect if eye contact is inappropriate in the family's culture) and to direct attention to all family members equally if more than one is present. Remind teachers to relax and smile—doing so sets a tone of friendly cooperation.

Ending the conference with a positive wrap-up

Remind teachers of the importance of a reassuring wrap-up such as "This meeting has been extremely helpful. We have a much better understanding of which strategies have worked for Neil in the past. We also have a great plan for supporting him at school. Let's check in with each other in two weeks to see how things are going. Thank you for meeting with us."

WHAT TO DO IF THINGS GET TENSE

Despite our best efforts, it's a reality that conferences sometimes get tense. Three strategies to teach staff for handling these situations are:

1. *Pause, breathe, and paraphrase*

Simply pausing and breathing can take the tension down a notch. After pausing and breathing, teachers should validate the parent's feelings and create shared understandings by paraphrasing the parent's concerns—while always keeping the focus on the child. For example, "It sounds like being fair to Val is a top priority that we all share."

2. Ask for time if needed

There's nothing wrong with asking for time to think or gather more information. For example, a teacher might say, "That's a very interesting point. We here at school should spend some time thinking about that. We'll do that and get back to you next week."

Sometimes, while asking for thinking time, it may be necessary for the teacher to remind parents about school rules or consequences that apply to their child. It's important to communicate this directly but respectfully. For example, "I'd like to spend some more time exploring that idea. But we need to let Val know that school rules say to keep everyone safe. We also have a school policy that when children hurt others, whether accidentally or intentionally, they will need to take a break at home."

3. End the conference if the tension becomes unmanageable

If anyone's feeling angry or very defensive, it's best that teachers end the conference and resume when all parties have had time to cool down. Respectful and direct language is again crucial: "We should continue this conversation, but I think it would be better to do that at another time."

Keep reminding teachers not to take it personally if a parent puts up walls or goes on the attack. Urge them to trust that the parent has the best of intentions and just wants their child to succeed in school.

If a Conference Is Needed, Be Involved From the Start

Even though most problem-solving conferences with parents will be called by a teacher, you should know that a conference is happening so you can offer support. For one thing, you should think about whether to come. A school leader's presence might give a teacher the courage to engage in a hard conversation. On the other hand, there could be situations in which it's best for teachers to speak without administrators at the table. Think about this issue case by case, and discuss it openly with the teacher.

Of course, to be involved, you need teachers to tell you when they're considering a conference. To help them feel safe doing this, reassure them that you consider it a sign of responsible teaching when they ask for your support. Then make sure your demeanor reinforces your words when they do come to you.

Beware the Surprise Factor

When our son was young, my husband and I were asked to come to school to talk about some attention issues our son was having. Tom and I arrived at what we thought was to be a conference with just his teacher, only to find the counselor and principal also in attendance. I immediately braced for difficult news. Throughout the conference, I was unable to take in much because I was so anxious. I made it through the meeting with a degree of poise, only to lose my cool in the parking lot afterward.

"Why're you so upset?" Tom asked. He pointed out that the school had shared strengths and some significant areas of growth in our son and offered ideas for further improvement, including things we were already doing at home. "I don't know! I was just not prepared for such a large group," I replied. "Things must be really serious if they all felt a need to come."

This experience taught me a great deal about what I call the "surprise factor." I learned that whenever school adults need to have a potentially difficult conversation with parents, even if it's about a fairly low-stakes issue, it's critical to eliminate surprises as much as possible.

If there will be additional people at a meeting, we need to let parents know ahead of time. If a school's policy is that a child who physically or verbally harms others will be required to take a break at home, parents need to be aware of this consequence before it is ever used. If a child is showing a pattern of problematic behaviors, the request for a conference should not be the first time the parent is hearing about the problem.

Eliminating the surprise factor goes a long way toward creating a safe environment for parents when hard truths must be discussed and school-home collaboration is desperately needed.

Don't Delay a Needed Conference

Keep in mind—and remind teachers—that small problems are easier to solve than big ones. So if a meeting with parents seems needed, it's important not to put it off. Delaying usually means allowing the problem to reach even more critical levels. At Riverwood Elementary in Memphis, Tennessee, principal Rita White requests a conference with parents the first time a teacher asks the administration for support or refers a child to the office. She invites parents to school for a meeting with the child's teacher and an administrator the following day.

Her goal, she explains, is to bring the parents on board as joint problem-solvers right from the get-go. The purpose of this early conference is for school adults to gather relevant information from parents, for school and home to articulate shared expectations of the child, and for everyone together to create a plan for supporting the child in meeting those expectations.

Note that acting early is not the same as rushing. Important discipline conversations should not be held in "fly-by conferences," those quick check-ins as parents pass by in the hallway—tempting as that is for busy school leaders and teachers. Scheduling a dedicated time to meet gives the conversation the time and focus it deserves.

Guide Teachers on How to Prepare for a Conference

Thorough preparation makes conferences more successful. Starting on the opposite page are the important preparatory steps in the form of a checklist that you can reproduce and pass out to teachers.

Preparing for a Conference

❑ **Carefully observe the child.**

Strengths: _____

_____

Problem areas: _____

_____

❑ **Describe the problem and goal in a nonjudgmental way.**

Problem: _____

_____

_____

_____

For example: "Maurice loves competitive sports, but he had to take a break from soccer last week because he slide tackled. When he re-entered the game today, he continued to slide tackle and inadvertently injured a classmate. We then had Maurice sit out the rest of the game," instead of "Maurice has terrible recess behavior. He's always too aggressive."

Goal: _____

_____

State the goal in positive terms. For example: "To help Maurice and others have a safe and fun experience" rather than "To help Maurice not hurt himself or others."

CONTINUED ON NEXT PAGE ▶

❏ **Consider who else should attend the meeting.**

_____

Think about:

- Whether a parent might be more comfortable if she or he brought someone, such as a relative, former teacher of the child, or other adult who has a good relationship with the child.

- Someone at school who's skillful with this particular behavior issue or close to the student and who could be of help in this conversation.

- A translator for the parents.

❏ **Let the parent know who will be present and what each person's role will be.**

❏ **Choose a location and time for the meeting.**

_____

Consider:

- School spaces that might be more relaxing for parents than the classroom— for example, the school library, family resource room, or counselor's office.

- Meeting after school hours at the child's home or other place in the community—better for parents with work schedules or transportation issues that make it hard for them to come to school during school hours.

❏ **Get adult-sized chairs for everyone.**

When you sit in a teacher-sized chair and have the parent sit in a student-sized chair, you communicate an uneven power relationship, which can immediately undermine the collaborative tone you're seeking.

Remind Teachers to Follow Up After a Conference

So that they get the most out of a conference, remind teachers to take these important follow-up steps:

- **Reflect with any colleagues who were at the meeting.** Were your school's hopes for the conference met? Was the tone respectful of parents and the student? What new information or insights did the teacher gain? If a plan of action was articulated at the end of the conference, does it align with your school's discipline principles and practices?

- **Send a follow-up note to parents.** The note should thank parents for attending the conference and summarize the main ideas discussed.

- **Check in with parents periodically.** Encourage teachers to continue checking in with parents to share the child's progress toward the goals named in the conference. In general, the more highly structured and intensive the support being given to the child, the more frequent these check-ins should be.

BABS REFLECTS

An Aikido Lesson for Schools

Even with the most thoughtful relationship-building with parents, school adults can sometimes be blindsided by an unexpected level of anger from a parent during a conversation. It takes skill to remain calm, de-escalate the situation, and move the parties toward greater understanding. I once received an introduction to the martial art of Aikido that taught me a lesson in this important skill.

Aikido employs the practice of "blending," which, as Aikido master George Burr Leonard explains, is meeting the energy that confronts you in a physical attack in such a way as to protect yourself and do no harm to the attacker (Leonard, 2000).

Just as when we're physically attacked, in the moment of receiving a verbal push from a parent, we have several choices. One choice is to push back, meeting a parent's anger with our own. For example, if a parent says, "Caleb told me that you were unfair! You always blame him for everything that goes wrong in the cafeteria. No wonder he acts up at lunch," we could reply, "I do not always blame him. We are NOT unfair, and he's got to learn to take responsibility for his actions!" This in essence shuts down communication and ignites already heated emotions.

Another choice is to fall back from the negative energy, assuming an attitude of denial or victimization and disengaging from the conversation. For example, we could say to the parent, "I'm sorry if he's feeling blamed. I didn't mean to make him feel that way," while being visibly upset and shaken.

The art and skill of blending, however, enables us to take a third course: to receive the negative energy, stay calm and centered, and empathize with the parent. "I can see it's important to you that Caleb is treated fairly at school. That's important to us, too. Our goal at this school is for all of the children to feel valued."

If the parent goes on to say angrily, "Caleb keeps telling me the other boys make fun of him. What do you expect him to do when everyone is always picking on him? He has a right to defend himself!" we can respond, "It sounds like teaching Caleb to defend himself in a way that doesn't hurt others needs to be a top priority. How can we work together to do that?"

The job of school leaders is to help staff learn the "blending" response to a parent's anger—to see the situation through the parent's eyes while reaching for a solution that helps the child and the rest of the school. Parents may not turn their negative energy around right away, but if school adults stay steady on this third blending choice, we can gradually steer the conversation toward a peaceful resolution and shape our school-home relationship into a more collaborative partnership.

FINAL THOUGHT

The Courage to Engage in High-Stakes Conversations

When students struggle, it takes parents and schools working together to fully support them. We need parents and they need us. Yes, it takes courage for school staff to engage in high-stakes conversations with parents. But school leaders can help staff find this courage. We begin by reminding staff that parents have positive intentions and simply want what's best for their child. We continue by giving staff practical tips for collaborative problem-solving with parents. And we always recognize staff's persistence in this hard and important work. Our guidance and encouragement make a world of difference.

PART THREE

Positive Behavior Everywhere

CHAPTER 12

Playground

SCHOOL LEADER'S CHECKLIST

❏ **Put recess before lunch if possible**

❏ **Provide ample and active adult supervision**

❏ **Spread recess duty among many adults**

    ❏ Consider giving the PE teacher oversight responsibility

❏ **Establish recess rules**

❏ **Teach and practice recess behaviors.** Involve:

    ❏ Classroom teachers

    ❏ PE teacher

    ❏ Recess supervisors

❏ **Teach free play**

❏ **Teach recess games**

❏ **Open play areas gradually**

❏ **Establish routines for starting and ending recess**

❏ **Communicate the plan for responding to misbehavior**

    ❏ Include a mini-course on positive adult language on the playground

Playground

Make recess a time of joy and learning

Recess is one of the most dynamic times of school, ripe with opportunities for children to enjoy physical activity and self-directed play, to connect with the natural world, to interact with a diverse peer group, and to practice essential social skills. The "curriculum" of recess includes weighty goals: developing children's social competencies and fostering their imaginations while meeting their need for safety, movement, and fun.

But recess can also be rife with opportunities for discipline problems. Consider all the sharing of equipment, choosing of teams, physical competition, and unstructured socializing that might go on during recess. Combine that with the often minimal adult supervision, and we have a perfect recipe for conflicts and resentments. These problems not only can spoil recess itself, but often carry over into the rest of the day.

So what do we do?

First of all, we keep recess. Some schools, feeling test-score pressure or fearing playground safety and liability issues, have eliminated this part of the school day. Eliminating recess will also get rid of all those discipline problems, the thinking sometimes goes.

But doing away with recess is one of the worst things we can do for children's academics, not to mention their health. And it won't improve behavior. Research has shown that when children have a break to run around outside, they're more attentive and on-task when they're inside (Jarrett, 2003; Barros, Silver, & Stein, 2009).

Recess is also crucial to children's development because it gives them time for free play. Researchers are learning that free play appears to be a genetically hardwired human need, one that children must satisfy if they're to become socially adept, and school recess is one of the few opportunities in many children's daily lives when they can meet this basic human need.

Even though children "play" soccer, kickball, and hopscotch, such organized games have preset rules. Free play doesn't; it therefore allows children to invent and test out ways to communicate, to be fair, to negotiate, to persist, and to solve problems. Free play also allows children to relieve stress. This kind of play is so important that some psychologists say limiting it can contribute to children's becoming anxious, socially maladjusted adults (Wenner, 2009; Ginsburg, 2007).

Many schools, districts, and states understand this and have instituted policies articulating the rights of children to participate in daily recess. For example, the state of Virginia, in its standards for accreditation of public schools, includes a requirement that "Each elementary school shall provide students with a daily recess during the regular school year as determined appropriate by the school" (Regulations Establishing Standards, 2006, p. 34).

After committing to keeping recess, school leaders need to take specific steps to make recess a safe, peaceful, enjoyable time for everyone. The following list of essential strategies is long, but not all these steps have to be taken at once. Start with one or two that seem most important for your school, get them working well, and then take on a few more. Each of these strategies is explained in detail in this chapter:

- Put recess before lunch if possible.

- Provide ample and active adult supervision.

- Establish recess rules.

- Teach and practice recess behaviors.

- Teach free play.

- Teach recess games.

- Open play areas gradually.

- Establish routines for starting and ending recess.

- Communicate the plan for responding to misbehavior.

- Pay attention to indoor recess.

A final word before we get into these strategies: Advise teachers not to keep children in from recess to make up missed work. Sitting out of recess for awhile may be an appropriate consequence for misbehaving at recess (so the child can regain self-control and recall recess rules), but it's not an appropriate consequence for work incompletion. Children need active play as much as they need food and sleep. If students need to complete missed work, teachers should look for a time during class for them to do that. One possibility is during academic choice period: While other children are doing the work of their choice, these children complete their assigned work.

Put Recess Before Lunch If Possible

If recess comes after lunch at your school, try switching them. This single step can significantly improve children's behavior. Exercising first and then eating fits how children's (and adults') bodies naturally work, and when children's physical needs are met, their behavior generally improves.

Four Corners Elementary School in Greenfield, Massachusetts, is just one of many schools that used the *Responsive School Discipline* approach to reorganize the middle of the day this way. After the school put recess ahead of lunch, the number of playground and lunchroom conflicts dropped, and the conflicts that did occur were more quickly mediated. In addition, says principal Gail Healy, "teachers immediately noticed a positive change in students' emotions and demeanor when they re-entered the classroom after lunch."

The "recess first" idea has gained national attention, with the U.S. Department of Agriculture and some states calling on schools to make the schedule switch (U.S. Department of Agriculture, 2000, p. 21; Wyoming Department of Education, n.d.; Montana Office of Public Instruction, 2009; Delisio, 2005).

Admittedly, it's not always possible to schedule recess before lunch for the whole school. But even if you can schedule this way for some of the grades, the overall middle-of-the-day climate is likely to improve.

Provide Ample and Active Adult Supervision

Having enough adults on the playground and giving these adults active roles sends an important message—to the children and the adults. To the children we're saying, "Kindness and respect are as important on the playground as in the classroom. The adults at school are going to help you be kind and respectful here, just as everywhere else at school." To the adults we're saying, "Teaching recess is just as important as teaching reading and math."

Four Corners Elementary used to have two adults at each recess supervising two entire grades, and the adults' role was limited to intervening when problems arose. When recess discipline problems pushed everyone's frustration levels up, the school, along with reversing the order of lunch and recess, added two more adults to playground duty.

Moreover, the adults each led a game or activity. Their role changed from reacting to crises to proactively teaching positive recess behavior. Discipline problems decreased. As Gail Healy put it, a few weeks after increasing the adult supervision "there was such a dramatic improvement in the quality of play and social interactions that we knew we were on the right track."

Here are ways to increase the adult presence at recess:

- **Spread recess duty among many adults, including administrators.** Not all schools can assign classroom teachers to recess every day. Nor can they hire additional staff. But with careful scheduling, it's possible to free up a few more adults to supervise on the playground. At Sheffield Elementary School in Turners Falls, Massachusetts, the principal and guidance counselor each had recess duty several times a week along with other staff. Leading a game like soccer or Capture the Flag was the principal's usual role. At Four Corners, the principal and the behavior management teacher joined recess whenever possible.

- **Make use of the PE teacher's expertise.** This doesn't have to mean giving the PE teacher daily recess duty. It can mean elevating this teacher's role to include oversight responsibility for the quality of recess. The PE teacher can train teachers or paraprofessionals in supervising the playground. One way they can do that is by teaching these adults games and activities that they can lead. Also have the PE teacher teach playground games to students as the first unit in the fall. When children come to recess knowing the structures and rules for lots of games and activities, their recess behavior improves.

No matter who's supervising recess, it's essential that the school leader establish the expectations for this time. It must be clear to all adults on the playground that their role is to actively supervise the children, not to socialize among themselves. A simple strategy that will help is to define different areas or zones on the playground and assign adults to supervise each area. This clear definition of space, which can be achieved by placing cones throughout the playground, will also create boundaries for the children and avoid some of the inevitable conflicts that occur when playing space is not well defined (such as tag games spilling over into the hopscotch area).

Establish Recess Rules

A school's recess rules should evolve from a shared understanding of its goals for this time of day. Your school can create a unique set of rules or apply schoolwide or classroom rules to recess (see Chapter 3). Either way, begin with the end in mind. Ask "Why is recess important? What is it we want children to learn at recess? What skills will students need if they're to play joyfully and safely?"

For example, at University School of Nashville, the PE department helped craft a general position statement about the nature of recess games. They named "good sportsmanship, teamwork, and cooperation" as aspects of play that the school strives to develop in children. "Games whose sole purpose is to eliminate players by striking them with a ball (for example, battle ball, dodge ball) do not embrace" these values, the statement said. About team selection when playing team games, the statement said, "Teams should be as equitable and fair as possible and should not be divided along gender or ability lines." The statement also encouraged teachers and recess aides to help children come up with other creative ways to form teams.

Later, when the school was ready to create playground rules, the process was easier because of the common vision articulated in the position statement. The final playground rules captured the values of sportsmanship, teamwork, and cooperation and additionally addressed a few specific safety issues. The final rules were:

- Play safely and take care of yourself and others.

- Rocks, sticks, and sand stay on the ground.

- Climb only on the inside of the wooden structure.

- Slide down the slide and use stairs for getting to the top.

Keep in mind that your school's recess rules, like all rules for common areas, need to be broad enough to be applied in developmentally appropriate ways to the whole range of ages in your school. For example, "Everyone can play," a common recess rule, works well because it embodies the important expectation of inclusiveness but translates to a variety of behavior expectations depending on the children's age. Other possible playground rules that are appropriately broad are:

- Use equipment and structures safely.

- Show teamwork and sportsmanship.

- Solve conflicts peacefully.

- Keep our playground clean.

Teach and Practice Recess Behaviors

Once playground rules are in place, we can't assume that children will know how to translate them into action. Instead, we need to teach this translation explicitly—intensively at the beginning of the year, and then again with extra reminders around vacations and holidays, when it's challenging for children to remember self-control.

Most often it's the classroom teachers who provide this instruction during the first few weeks of school, but it's the school leader's responsibility to set the expectation that teachers will do this teaching. It's also the school leader's responsibility to make sure adults' expectations for playground behavior are consistent throughout the school. Giving the PE teacher oversight responsibility for the quality of recess, as described earlier, can help ensure this consistency.

Here are important leadership actions for achieving consistent and quality teaching of recess behaviors at your school:

- **Plan who will do this teaching, when, and how.** Begin planning before the end of the previous year, and involve the entire staff. For example, in April or May, make the next fall's recess teaching a topic of an all-staff meeting.

- **Plan for all recess adults to be present at the teaching of recess behaviors.** If at all possible, have all adults who will be supervising recess be with classroom teachers in the classrooms, or with the PE teacher on the playground, when behavior expectations are being taught. If this can't happen due to scheduling conflicts, meet with the recess supervisors separately to explain the expectations for behavior—and provide instruction in how to respond to misbehavior.

- **Take the lead in teaching recess yourself.** By doing some of the actual teaching, school leaders convey to staff the importance of this teaching while demonstrating effective techniques. One method you can use is to give groups of students, accompanied by their teacher, a tour of the recess space on or near the first day of school. During the tour, teach students how to follow one recess rule. Later, in classrooms, teachers can continue teaching the other recess rules.

- **Urge the use of interactive modeling.** It's impossible to overstate the importance of going into detail when teaching recess rules, and interactive modeling is a great method for ensuring that this detailed teaching happens. Support teachers in using interactive modeling with fidelity. (See Chapter 5 for more information.) You can also use interactive modeling yourself when you teach recess rules.

- **Be explicit about which behaviors need to be modeled.** Give staff a list of routines or procedures that they should cover when teaching recess behaviors (or involve staff in generating a list together). This level of specificity is key to consistency among all adults and to the children's success. (See "Recess Behaviors to Teach" on page 180 for details.)

■ **Lead a "recess" for adults.** At a staff meeting early in the year, take the staff outside for a mock recess that they participate in. Lead the recess, modeling how to teach positive recess behaviors. Once back inside, lead the staff in reflecting on what they experienced outside and how they can use those teaching techniques with their students.

■ **Use reinforcing language when children show positive recess behaviors.** Encourage all staff to do the same. A great time to do this is during lineup at the end of recess before the children go inside. "People shared the hula hoops today like we practiced." "I heard a lot of people complimenting each other on good plays out there." "You stopped and waited calmly until it was your turn, Chris." Such language is powerful. When adults name the cooperative, friendly playing they see, students are likely to continue showing those behaviors. (See page 52 in Chapter 4 for more about reinforcing language.)

RECESS BEHAVIORS TO TEACH

Here are some of the most common behaviors that need to be modeled to make recess successful. There may be many others specific to your school. Share your list with all teachers so that all students learn these routines and procedures.

■ How to line up

■ How to circle up

■ How to respond to the signal (make sure your signal is loud enough for students to hear on a noisy playground)

■ What to do if a child gets hurt (one protocol that works well is to have students quickly make a circle around an injured child until an adult arrives, reassuring the child that a grownup is coming but not touching the child)

■ What to do if an adult tells you to take a break or to change activities

■ What to do if a ball or other equipment goes out of bounds

Teach Free Play

"Teach free play" may sound like a contradiction, but it's actually one of the most important, and most overlooked, aspects of teaching recess. Even when children are playing freely, they need to play with control. Recess rules, which ensure safety and kindness, still apply. And children still need to *feel* safe. So although the teaching of free play can be brief, it cannot be skipped.

Following is an example of how this teaching might look for a group of fourth graders. (These steps can be done by a classroom teacher, PE teacher, or school leader.)

Inside a classroom, the adult leads students in brainstorming what kinds of imaginative play the children might invent on the playground. The class then goes outside. "See that tree line over there?" the adult asks the group. "It's okay to go over there and play. Let's all walk over there and take a look." The children notice the bumps in the ground made by the tree roots. They see that the trees' lower branches are low enough to climb on. One child looks for poison ivy, which he has recently learned to identify.

"There'll always be a teacher here to keep you safe," the adult says. Adult presence is crucial. We must give children the space to play as they like, but we cannot leave them unattended. "You can play at whatever you want to here, as long as you keep your body safe and follow our other recess rules," the teacher continues. She then briefly reviews the rules with them and demonstrates how to follow those rules when hanging and swinging from a low tree branch, when gathering twigs to make boundaries for an improvised game, and so forth. Finally, she asks student volunteers to demonstrate what following the rules looks and sounds like when doing other activities in the free play area.

In subsequent days back in the classroom, the class role-plays ways to solve exclusion problems that can arise in free play—before such problems actually come up. Then, when they do come up, as they inevitably will, the children will have a repertoire of solutions to try.

In this way, we watch over the children while honoring their freedom.

Teach Recess Games

At the same time as teaching free play, we need to give children a repertoire of fun, safe games to play at recess. Kensington Avenue School in Springfield, Massachusetts, demonstrates the necessity and power of teaching playground games.

Located in an urban area, Kensington's playground consists of a blacktop. No basketball hoop, no jungle gym, no swings, no ball field. Without such structures to support them in safe independent play, the children have a special need for adults to teach them blacktop games.

So every day at Kensington, when a class goes out to recess, their teacher or an assistant accompanies them. In the first weeks of school, the adults carefully teach tag games, hopscotch, hula hoops, and jump rope to the kindergartners through third graders, and kickball and other ball games to the fourth and fifth graders. As the children get familiar with the games, the adults join in or actively supervise the play, which keeps the children physically safe and helps them feel emotionally secure. The result is a climate of safety, kindness, and playfulness.

Of course, the need to teach recess games is not limited to schools with small or sparsely equipped recess spaces. Even on playgrounds that have ample play structures and recess supplies, many children don't know what to do during recess. They may not be ready for the social navigation needed for unstructured play with peers, or they may be hesitant to join the highly competitive and physically rough games that sometimes dominate recess. Teaching recess games is therefore critical at all schools.

Here are some recommendations for this teaching:

- **Set the tone by teaching some recess games yourself.** You can convey how committed you are to improving recess by teaching a new playground game yourself once in awhile. Doing so not only sends a powerful message to both the children and the adults at school but also models for staff how to teach games.

- **Teach the rules even for common games.** Remind staff that many games that we think are well known may be confusing to some children. So adults should deliberately teach all game rules and allow some "no pressure" practice before playing for real to give children a chance to build confidence and mastery. As the year goes on, teachers should continue to review, as needed, the rules of games that students commonly play before the class goes out to recess.

■ **Remind children that general recess rules always apply.** Make sure staff frequently reinforce for children that the overall rules for recess always apply, no matter what game they're playing. Additionally, they should teach students how to show good sportsmanship, such as by forming teams in fair and kind ways and recognizing the efforts of the losing team.

■ **Teach tag rules.** Since tag will be played so often, be sure children learn rules that apply to all tag games, such as "Tagger's choice" (the tagger is always right, even if his or her tag was so soft that it wasn't felt), "Limited time on safety" (children count to five or ten and then must leave), and "No babysitting" (a tagger must stand five paces away from safety while the player on safety counts).

■ **Modify game rules to keep the play fun and safe.** For starters, institute tagging instead of tackling in football and make aggressive moves illegal in soccer. Observe to see what additional rule changes are needed at your school.

■ **Emphasize fun and cooperation rather than winning.** For example, in games involving teams and scores, encourage staff to have scorers switch sides after scoring for their teams, or add the final scores of both teams and challenge students to beat that total score the next day. If you notice unhealthy competition creeping into playground games, prompt teachers to talk with their classes about it and engage the children in brainstorming for solutions. To make playground cooperation fun, you can surprise the whole school by announcing a "Wacky Relays Tournament" and asking the children for their ideas on how they can help everyone have fun no matter who wins.

■ **Reflect with children after teaching a game.** Help teachers see the value of gathering the class for five minutes after the recess and lunch break to ask "What made your games fun during recess today?" Show them how to probe for deep understanding. For example, if students say "We cooperated," teachers can ask "What do you mean by 'cooperated'?" and ask students to name examples.

(For recess game ideas, see *36 Games Kids Love to Play* by Adrian Harrison, available from www.responsiveclassroom.org, and *6 Steps to a Trouble-Free Playground* by Curt Hinson, available from www.playfiteducation.com.)

Open Play Areas Gradually

If your school has a play structure, basketball area, or other specialized play spaces, make them closed to children when school opens in the fall. During the first days of school, have adults take the children one class at a time to each play area and guide the children in exploring each part of it, discussing, demonstrating, and letting children practice its potential uses. "What's one safe way to play on the monkey bars? Who would like to show us?" "What's another possible way to play safely here? Who wants to show that?" Provide a language "cheat sheet" if you need to so that all the adults use consistent language. Open the structure or area only after this guided exploration.

Safety, of course, is a top reason for doing this gradual opening. Other important reasons are that it stretches children to invent and try different ways to play, instills the importance of being fair and caring, and encourages them to value the equipment, all of which translate to a more fun and peaceful recess for all.

Older children sometimes complain about having to endure this slow opening of play areas year after year. Their complaining may be a way to show that they're grown up. The truth, however, is that some older students may still need a reminder about how to use the equipment.

Also, children change as they age: At five, they may be learning how to use a playground structure for the first time. At ten, they may be wanting to climb on the very top of it or to do fancy flips off of it. At each age, they'll need demonstrations and reminders of how to use the structure in a way that's fun and challenging for them, yet safe and considerate.

So stick to your agenda while validating older children's feeling of maturity. "I know you know this stuff, but it's important that everyone understands our rules." Or, even better, enlist these students to come to younger classes' guided explorations to help demonstrate the proper use of the spaces.

Establish Routines for Starting and Ending Recess

Transitions are tone setters. If students transition into recess well, many recess problems will be prevented. If they transition out of recess well, many problems during the following period will be prevented. And when recess goes well, the rest of the day goes better, too.

So begin recess at your school with a brief routine that helps children shift calmly from classroom mode to recess mode. The routine should allow the children to take a moment to decide what to play and remind themselves of the recess rules. The routine should also give recess supervisors time to make safety announcements or give brief reminders about the rules.

At Sheffield Elementary in Turners Falls, Massachusetts, recess begins with all students circling up on the blacktop. The lead recess teacher raises a hand to signal for quiet. When the children are attentive, the teacher introduces the day's playground activities. "Today's field activity is kickball. We'll have a game of Knock-Out on this side of the basketball court and Four Square on the other. And we've added longer jump ropes to the equipment cart today. OK, all set?" "All set!" the children respond. "ALL SET?" the teacher calls out again. "YOU BET!" the children chorus. Then they quickly go off to play.

On days when the children need it, the lead recess teacher also takes this time to give a brief reminder about recess social skills: "Who can share a fair solution if two people want to be in the same place on the play structure at the same time?" Children respond, "Rock, Paper, Scissors" or "Take turns."

Some days require a special safety announcement: "It's very windy today. You need to be able to hear teachers calling you in, so we're going to bring the playing area boundaries to the orange cones." All this takes just two minutes, but it makes a world of difference to the children's behavior.

Twenty minutes later, at the end of recess, another routine helps the students shift calmly back to indoor mode. The lead recess teacher calls, "Allie, Allie!" The children, who've practiced responding to this signal since day one of school, come in from the field, return equipment to the cart, line up by class on the blacktop, and watch for a recess teacher's raised-hand quiet signal.

The recess teacher then gives them some quick reinforcing feedback about positive recess behavior observed and a brief calming activity—a song or rhythm game for younger children and short mental math problems for older students. Then, the classroom teachers escort their classes into the building.

Remember, recess start and end routines will be most successful if all adults teach and use them as carefully and deliberately as all other school routines.

Communicate the Plan for Responding to Misbehavior

It's critical for every adult who has a role in supervising recess to understand the school's protocol for responding to misbehavior and to know how this protocol should look on the playground. Specifically, all supervisors need to know:

- **How to respond to a conflict.** For example, one method might be that the adult offers help in resolving the conflict, but if it can't be resolved quickly, the adult tells the children to play in separate areas and reports the problem to the classroom teacher, who will help the children problem-solve later in the day.

- **When to tell a child to take a break and where the child should go.** For example, two possibilities for a take-a-break spot are next to the adult and at a designated spot (such as a picnic table) that is easily seen by the adults present.

- **How to release a child from take-a-break.** Help all recess supervisors learn and practice using a matter-of-fact and friendly manner and giving a brief reminder about the behavior that's expected. For example, "OK, Alexa, come back in the game. Remember, gentle tagging."

- **What to do if a child refuses to follow a direction.** Decide how recess supervisors are to enlist help, such as from your school's chain of support, for minor problems. Communicate this plan to all recess supervisors.

- **When and how to activate the school's crisis team in the event of major problems.** Make sure all recess supervisors know who's on the crisis team and how to activate their help. Frequently review this information with them.

In addition, since so often adults will be responding to misbehavior on the playground with a brief reminder or redirection, it's critical that you provide supervisors with a mini-course on positive adult language on the playground (see Chapter 4 for a comprehensive discussion of positive adult language). Even one hour of training with you or a lead teacher demonstrating effective ways to talk to students (with real-life examples from the playground, such as two children grabbing the same ball or a child beginning to wander beyond the boundaries), will produce positive results. Emphasize the importance of tone in these examples. Demonstrate how the same words delivered using various tones will send vastly different messages.

Also, make sure you emphasize the importance of being aware of how one's body language can affect children, especially when they're excited or agitated. Often at recess, adults can inadvertently cause a child's negative behavior to escalate by doing the following:

- Getting too close to a child

- Pointing a finger at a child

- Pulling something out of a child's hand

- Raising their voice

- Gritting their teeth or scowling

Finally, invite recess supervisors to come to you with their observations about the playground throughout the year. The adults who are on the playground every day often have the best ideas about how to improve recess. Don't forget to ask their advice!

Pay Attention to Indoor Recess

The principles described above for teaching recess and opening recess options slowly apply to indoor recess as well. Students need to be taught—through interactive modeling, role-playing, and positive adult language—how to apply classroom and recess rules to indoor recess. And board games and other indoor activities should be introduced carefully before they're opened to students.

One wintry day when ice made playing in the schoolyard unsafe, a fourth grade class at Kensington Avenue School in Springfield, Massachusetts, was moving from math to indoor recess. Within a minute, the children settled into small groups at tables. At one table, three students played Scrabble with their teacher. At another, two friends engaged in a simplified form of Yahtzee. At yet another table, a circle of children played cards. The room filled with a contented buzz, punctuated by giggles and laughter. After twenty minutes, at a signal and a word from their teacher, the children put their games away and lined up to go to lunch.

This relaxed orderliness was possible only because indoor recess was carefully taught, practiced, supervised, and revised as needed.

CHIP REFLECTS

Remember to Have Fun

Recess is supposed to be fun. Sadly, many children are under so much stress from school or home life, or both, that they're not having much fun anymore, not even at recess. In my forty years in education, I've observed multitudes of children. In recent years the light seems to have gone out of many children's eyes.

It's up to us adults to help bring that light back. We can allow children to revive or retain their sense of fun while we teach behavior expectations. The message is "Everyone can have the most fun when we all stay within the rules." We school leaders can set this positive tone. Turn mundane tasks like lining up into "beat the clock" challenges. Inject little surprises like having children line up in reverse alphabetical order. Say simple things like "That looks like fun!" Laugh. A little playfulness helps lighten the mood for children—and ourselves.

FINAL THOUGHT

Check In Regularly With Staff

Throughout the year, regularly ask staff how things are going with recess. Make time at staff meetings to surface problems, or set up separate times to check in. Are games getting too aggressive? Are children confused about equipment? Then make needed adjustments to the structure and teaching of recess. Even small changes can make a difference. For example, Sheffield Elementary staff came up with the idea of having the younger grades sit during their brief circling-up at the start of recess as an additional way to help them stay calm and listen. Just that minor tweak improved the children's attention.

These staff check-ins can be brief. The important thing is to have them, to include all the recess adults, and to revise recess practices and policies as needed according to what you learn.

Cafeteria

SCHOOL LEADER'S CHECKLIST

❑ **Look for traffic jams**

❑ **Establish cafeteria rules**

❑ **Teach and practice cafeteria behaviors.** Involve:

   ❑ Classroom teachers

   ❑ Lunch supervisors

   ❑ Kitchen staff

❑ **Provide training to all cafeteria staff.** Include instruction in:

   ❑ Lunchtime rules

   ❑ Using the signal for quiet attention

   ❑ Appropriate adult language

   ❑ How to respond to misbehavior

❑ **Involve cafeteria supervisors and kitchen staff in problem-solving**

❑ **Teach children simple activities for wait times**

❑ **Consider having teachers assign lunch partners**

Cafeteria

Create a calm, pleasant lunchtime

Lunchtime can be a rich experience for students, with purposes beyond allowing them to eat. This part of the school day is an opportunity for children to enjoy their friends, make new friends, relax and recharge for the afternoon's lessons, try out social skills, and practice making choices for everything from food to conversation topics. Additionally, lunchtime holds great potential for enhancing the overall school climate, since children tend to carry lunchtime moods and dynamics with them into the rest of their school day.

On the flip side, children need a lot of skills if they're to navigate lunch well and derive all these benefits. If lunch is truly going to be a pleasant experience for all, school adults need to explicitly teach many skills, including how to wait patiently in line, how to respond if you don't like a food choice, and what to do when you're done eating.

Given that lunchtime is potentially rewarding and, for many students, hard, schools would be wise to put significant effort into ensuring that this time of the day goes well. If lunchtime at your school could use improvement, start by leading one or two changes. Even after some small reforms, success can spark enthusiasm among the school community to do more.

This chapter discusses these important strategies for improving lunchroom discipline:

- Look for traffic jams.

- Establish cafeteria rules.

- Teach and practice cafeteria behaviors.

- Provide training to all cafeteria staff.

- Involve cafeteria supervisors and kitchen staff in problem-solving.

- Teach children simple activities for wait times.

Look for Traffic Jams

Imagine a crowded grocery store. Shoppers try to squeeze by each other in the narrow aisles. You just want a box of pasta, but a knot of carts blocks your way. A cart bumps you from behind. Annoyance rises. Tempers flare.

The same thing happens daily in many school cafeterias. Too many children need to get to too many places all at once. The hot food line is moving too slowly; those who just want milk have to cut through it. And there's a traffic jam at the trash and recycle bins. Everyone's patience is tried, and behavior goes downhill.

If lunchtime discipline at your school isn't what you'd like it to be, see if bad traffic flow could be a culprit. That's what leaders of Bristol Elementary School in Vermont did. After observing the traffic congestion, they rerouted the hot lunch line, relocated the trash cans, and moved the condiments to separate stations away from the food line.

Combined with some procedural changes, these simple steps made lunch a more pleasant time for students and adults. Teachers also noticed students transitioning more smoothly from lunch back to their classrooms.

"But our cafeteria is a converted room. It's a tough space to work with, and we can't change the layout," many schools say. That's perfectly understandable. It's a frustrating fact that many of our schools were built without consultation with educators or are buildings originally designed for other purposes. We're stuck with what we've got.

But that makes it even more important to improve traffic flow and layout wherever we can. Even small changes, like Bristol's solution of moving trash cans and condiment stations, can make a noticeable difference. Start by observing a few lunch periods and noting any congestion. Traffic and procedural solutions often begin suggesting themselves once we stop to take a close look.

Establish Cafeteria Rules

Having cafeteria rules that everyone in school is familiar with anchors all the rest of your school's work on lunchtime discipline. Two ways to establish cafeteria rules are to:

- Create a set of cafeteria-specific rules.

- Apply schoolwide or classroom rules.

Creating a set of cafeteria-specific rules

To use this option, start by leading your school in articulating clear goals for lunch and a set of positive behaviors that will allow all the children to achieve these goals. At Egypt Elementary in Memphis, Tennessee, the school's *Responsive Classroom* Core Team met in late summer, before school opened, to launch this work. The team, comprising a teacher representative from each grade and two administrators, agreed upon this vision for the lunchroom: Children will have a dining experience that teaches them important social skills, skills that serve them well at school, at the family dining table, and in restaurants.

The team then brainstormed the positive behaviors one would see if such a vision were realized. After sorting and consolidating their list (see Chapter 3 for details about this process), they came up with the following cafeteria rules, all stated in the positive:

- Remain seated at tables.

- Eat appropriately.

- Keep hands and feet to yourself to keep others safe.

- Use quiet voices and speak in a conversational tone.

- Speak and act respectfully to adults and children.

Teachers' contracts at Egypt Elementary stipulate a duty-free lunch, and paraprofessionals supervise the cafeteria. However, with enthusiastic encouragement from the Core Team, the teachers volunteered to eat lunch with their classes during the first three weeks of school so they could teach and guide students in practicing the lunch rules. This also enabled the teachers to model positive adult language and positive adult-student interactions for the lunch supervisors.

Applying schoolwide or classroom rules

Some schools, instead of creating a set of rules specifically for the lunchroom, choose to apply their schoolwide rules, posting them in the lunchroom in addition to elsewhere throughout the building.

Or, as at Bush Hill Elementary in Alexandria, Virginia, students are taught to apply their classroom rules to the lunchroom. Both are effective options. At Bush Hill, in addition to teachers modeling and practicing with students what their classroom rules would look and sound like in the cafeteria, students bring a poster of their classroom rules with them to the cafeteria each day and hang these "traveling rules" on the end of their table as a behavior reminder.

Teach and Practice Cafeteria Behaviors

It's important that we not assume children know how to translate the cafeteria rules into action. Instead, we need to teach them how—by modeling expected behaviors and guiding the children in practicing them. And we need to cover all the essential cafeteria skills that children will need.

Who should do this teaching?

Give all classroom teachers and as many lunchroom adults as possible a role in this teaching. Not only is this a practical way to make sure all students get the teaching, but it lets students see all the adults teaching and reinforcing the same expectations. They get a clear message that all the adults at their school care about the lunchroom climate and all the adults respect children enough to set them up for success.

Also be sure to take an active role in the teaching yourself. For example, you can launch the teaching of cafeteria behaviors and then have classroom teachers continue on with more detailed teaching. At Kensington Avenue

School in Springfield, Massachusetts, *Responsive Classroom* facilitator Sheree Nolley meets with each grade's students and teachers in the lunchroom at the beginning of the year. She introduces the lunchroom rules and procedures and their purpose ("so that everyone can have a relaxed and safe lunch period"). After this introduction, the classroom teachers teach their own classes the specifics of the lunchroom rules and procedures.

When and how should this teaching be done?

Cafeteria rules and expected behavior should be taught intensively during the first few weeks of school, just as with expectations for all the other times and places in school. Here are some keys to making this teaching effective:

- **Go into detail, using interactive modeling.** Remind staff to err on the side of modeling more rather than less. You might give them, or engage them in creating, a list of procedures and routines to teach. (See "Cafeteria Behaviors to Teach" on page 196 for a suggested list.) Teaching in detail doesn't have to take an inordinate amount of time, since many skills and procedures can be modeled in only a few minutes.

- **Do the teaching in the cafeteria.** Children understand lunchtime expectations better if they see the expectations modeled right in the cafeteria. Teachers can begin a discussion of positive lunchroom behaviors in the classroom, but then they should take the class to the cafeteria—at a time of day when the place is quiet and free of distractions—to model and have students practice each of the behaviors they discussed. You can support this method by scheduling the cafeteria visits.

- **Involve lunchroom supervisors in teaching cafeteria behavior.** Involving lunchroom staff ensures consistency in adult expectations. It also helps the children build a respectful relationship with these adults. At Garfield Elementary School in Springfield, Virginia, Ms. Khan, the head lunchroom supervisor, visited each classroom to talk about what the students would like lunchtime to look and feel like. She then worked with a group of student leaders to design appropriate cafeteria rules. Later, when the children were practicing these rules, Ms. Khan was there with them, taking part in the interactive modeling. Regardless of how your school decides to involve lunchroom supervisors in teaching lunch, be sure they have significant roles that are visible to the children.

- **Redouble efforts around vacations and holidays.** Ask teachers to reteach lunchroom expectations and give extra reminders and reinforcing comments during these times of the year (and do some of the reteaching yourself). For example, teachers can talk about lunchtime during morning meetings or hold problem-solving discussions about cafeteria behavior if needed. Classes can role-play cafeteria situations, with a few students gathered around a table in the classroom holding a "lunch table conversation" while the rest of the class observes and then offers comments.

- **Encourage teachers to accompany their classes to lunch sometimes.** You can occasionally eat with students as well. This is especially important around vacations and holidays, when children need extra guidance on behavior. Sometimes the adult doesn't even need to say anything. Her presence by itself is often enough to remind students of behavior expectations.

CAFETERIA BEHAVIORS TO TEACH

Here's a list—no doubt partial—of the specific skills that we need to teach children if they're to have, and allow everyone else to have, a good lunch period. To this starter list, add any procedures that are particular to your school, such as how to pick up and hand in lunch tickets or, if you have picnic-style tables with attached benches, how to safely climb into or out of them while carrying a tray. Give your final list to all teachers so that the teaching of cafeteria behaviors is consistent throughout the school.

Here's the starter list of cafeteria skills:

- Waiting in line

- Passing in line, if passing is allowed

- Selecting foods (make sure to address what children should do if they don't like a food choice)

- Carrying a lunch tray safely

- Opening food containers

- Disposing of trash responsibly

- Showing respect to lunch servers and fellow students (saying thank you, what to say if you don't like something that is being served or that another student is eating, and so forth)

- Selecting a place to sit

- Choosing appropriate conversation topics

- Welcoming and greeting others when joining a table

- What to do when finished eating

- Showing basic table manners and dining etiquette (how to use utensils, what to do if you burp, keeping your mouth closed when chewing, waiting to talk until your mouth is empty, and so forth)

- Knowing the universal sign of choking and what to do if you see it (go get an adult immediately)

Provide Training to All Cafeteria Staff

If all the adults at school are to be consistent in their expectations and practices around discipline, we need to offer relevant training to all of them. When it comes to lunchtime, it's essential that any adult who interacts with students in the cafeteria get training in the following:

- What the cafeteria rules are

- How to effectively use the signal for quiet attention

- How to talk to students (give the basics of positive adult language and illustrate with various lunchroom scenarios, including those involving children who often struggle with behavior)

- What to do if a child misbehaves (establish clear expectations for how to respond if a child or group of children is showing inappropriate behavior; model reminding and redirecting language)

- When and how to activate your school's chain of support to seek help from colleagues, and how to activate the crisis team in case of a major problem

An example

An example of staff training in lunchtime discipline comes from Kensington Avenue School, the Massachusetts school mentioned previously. Kensington offered professional development in positive adult language to its lunch aides as well as to the kitchen staff. The goal was to ensure that these staff members, called "lunch teachers" at Kensington, used the same signals and language that teachers were using effectively in the classrooms.

The training began with a mini-workshop early in the school year. The lunch teachers came to school early that day and received their regular wage for this extra time. Tina Valentine, then head teacher, showed them how to use the all-school signal for attention and how to use positive reinforcing, reminding, and redirecting language to guide children's behavior.

After the workshop, Ms. Valentine modeled using these techniques in the lunchroom and observed the lunch teachers using them. After a few weeks, she met with them to reflect on how things were going and then provided one-on-one coaching throughout the year as needed.

In the following years, a similar workshop was offered every fall at Kensington. Both returning and new staff were invited. As the years went on, the more experienced lunch teachers began mentoring the new ones, helping to model and coach as the positive communication techniques became more and more rooted in the lunchroom culture.

Take-a-break (positive time-out) in the cafeteria

Often when misbehaviors are just beginning during lunch, a short break in the action can help. Make sure all the adults and students understand the protocol for using take-a-break in the lunchroom. Designating a few stand-alone desks or a small table that's reserved for students who need to take a break will be helpful.

In cases when an entire table of students is beginning to be disruptive, such as by talking too loudly or banging on the table, the entire group can be calmly but firmly told to "take a quick time-out" by pushing their trays to the center of the table and sitting quietly with their hands on top of the table for a minute or two. Suggest this strategy to lunchroom adults, and of course be sure students are taught and have practiced this routine ahead of time. It's also important that the adult who releases the students know to offer a brief and matter-of-fact reminder about lunchroom expectations: "Remember our rule about being quiet with our voices and our bodies so that everyone can have a pleasant lunch."

ASSIGNING LUNCH PARTNERS

Consider having teachers assign children lunch partners as an additional way to make lunch a positive social experience and to prevent cliques and exclusions. Here are some ideas for forming pairs:

- **Random pairings.** The teacher or students draw name cards. If students draw, the drawing order should change each day (for example, draw in alphabetical name order one day, by birth order the next day, etc.).

- **Pairings by commonality.** Children with the same initials, wearing shirts of the same color, or reading the same book sit together that day. If the teacher assigns these pairs, children can have fun guessing what their commonality is.

- **Category invitations.** After the children have had some practice eating with lunch partners, they can invite their own partners based on categories their teacher names—for example, invite someone who has the same pet as you. After further practice, the children can come up with their own categories. To keep students from picking and choosing to get their best friend or the "popular" classmates, teachers can create a rule, such as "Your partner has to be someone you haven't eaten with in the past two weeks."

Regardless of how children find lunch partners, it's important that teachers teach them how to extend and accept invitations graciously and how to behave in friendly ways toward their partners during lunch.

One word of caution: Remind teachers not to overdo partner lunches. It's best to intersperse partner days with free-choice days (with the understanding that all students are still responsible for making sure all classmates feel safe and welcomed).

Involve Cafeteria Supervisors and Kitchen Staff in Problem-Solving

If there's a problem in the cafeteria, whom better to turn to for solutions than the cafeteria supervisors and kitchen staff? These adults are in the cafeteria every day and see details of the activity there that other adults don't. They may therefore think of solutions that elude others. Inviting these adults' ideas also encourages their investment in building a positive cafeteria climate and helps everyone at school see them as an integral part of the school community.

Bristol Elementary, the Vermont school mentioned above, offers an example. In addition to observing that the locations of the food line, condiments, and trash cans were less than ideal, school leaders noticed that the children were having a hard time deciding among the many food choices offered in the food line, causing the line to slow to a standstill. After they discussed the problem with the kitchen staff, the kitchen manager simplified some menus, and the line began to flow more efficiently. That helped improve the children's behavior.

Teach Children Simple Activities for Wait Times

Even in the relatively short half hour of a typical lunch period, there are times when children have to wait: for their table to be called to go to the hot food line, for a slow-moving line to inch forward, for the end of the lunch period to arrive if they finish eating early. Waiting breeds boredom, and boredom often breeds behavior problems.

Although we can't eliminate wait times, schools can guide children in doing simple, positive activities to amuse themselves while waiting. Here are some easy, effective ideas to try at your school:

- **Have students bring a book or puzzle.** Encourage teachers of the older grades in your school to have their students bring a favorite book or puzzle so they'll have something to do if they finish eating early. (This usually isn't an issue with younger students, who typically eat more slowly.)

■ **Teach simple games.** Hand-clapping games and games involving tapping and passing empty cups or milk cartons around a table in set patterns are good choices. Children can become extremely engaged in these games—and get practice in math, music, and language arts without even realizing it. Ask your school's music teacher to create and teach patterns for these games. Better yet, have the children come up with their own patterns and teach them to their class or at an all-school gathering.

■ **Provide conversation starter cards.** Use student-level trivia cards, or invite teachers to have their students make cards (for example, "Facts about Our School" cards or cards on content they're studying). A card such as "Snakes always keep their eyes open, even when they are asleep. If you could be any reptile, which reptile would you be? Why?" could spark conversations that amuse children while allowing them to practice classification, science, and language arts skills.

CHIP REFLECTS

When We Eat in the Cafeteria Ourselves

The school cafeteria, as we all know, is traditionally a place that teachers try to avoid at all costs. Teachers need to have breaks in their day, and giving teachers duty-free lunch periods on most days allows them to have this break. But what if teachers saw the cafeteria as a place where they might go on some days to enjoy lunch in the company of students and even other teachers? What would it take for them to see the lunchroom this way?

Visible leadership from school leaders—that's what I believe it takes. It's extremely powerful when the principal invites a student to be her lunch partner and everyone sees the two of them eating together in the cafeteria. Many principals set up a "principal's lunch table" once a week. Why not hold these in the cafeteria rather than in the principal's office? When other adults at school see leaders enjoying the lunchroom, they're more likely to view the place with new eyes—as a place worthy of students and adults. And with that comes investment in keeping it a pleasant place.

You can also encourage students to invite teachers and other staff to eat with them from time to time. Or have an occasional "ask an outside adult to lunch" week, when children can invite their parent, another relative, or any adult in their life. Find other creative ways to invite adult guests into the lunchroom. The more adults see the cafeteria as a place to enjoy themselves rather than a place to avoid, the better the lunchroom climate will be.

FINAL THOUGHT

Try Round Tables

One final strategy for improving cafeteria discipline, for schools that can consider changing their lunchroom furniture, is to replace the traditional long tables with round ones. The shape allows students to see each other more easily and converse without shouting. When the noise level goes down, often the tension goes down as well.

Round tables also help foster a sense of community. We have children sit in a circle for meetings and many lessons so everyone can see everyone else. We use circles because they put everyone in an equal position and encourage inclusion of all. Using round tables in the lunchroom would reinforce this same feeling of community.

Hallways

SCHOOL LEADER'S CHECKLIST

❑ **Establish hallway rules**

❑ **Specify age-appropriate behavior expectations**

   ❑ Ask teachers to invite student input on how safe they feel in the hallways and how they would like the hallways to sound and look

   ❑ Discuss with adults at a staff meeting

❑ **Teach hallway expectations and routines to students.** Involve:

   ❑ Classroom teachers

   ❑ Other staff who are likely to be in the hallways, such as custodians

❑ **Create orderly and friendly arrival and dismissal routines**

❑ **Increase adult presence in the hallways during busy transition times such as arrival and dismissal.** Consider having:

   ❑ Hallway greeters welcome children as they enter the building

   ❑ Teachers walk students to the bus area

❑ **Be present in the hallways yourself, especially during arrival and dismissal times**

❑ **Determine, and communicate to staff, procedures for handling problems.** Be sure all staff know how to respond to children who are breaking rules, upset, or unsupervised in the hall.

Hallways

Keep them orderly and friendly

Hallways present unique challenges to school discipline. Unlike in other shared school spaces like the cafeteria, playground, or bus, in hallways it's often hard to predict which children will be there and with whom they will be interacting. Students could be by themselves or with their class or teacher, and they could encounter individual peers, another class, school staff, or visitors. Students can also be traveling the hallways for different purposes, feeling different emotions.

Given all these variables, how do we make sure children feel safe and maintain at least reasonable behavior in hallways? What's "reasonable" hallway behavior anyway? Do all the adults at school picture the same things? If students aren't feeling safe or aren't managing their conduct in the hallways, why aren't they? Do we know if there's hallway bullying taking place? Are we providing enough transition time between classes and between recess and lunch?

These are important questions because negative school hallway experiences affect students' willingness to trust and their ability to learn. Positive hallway experiences, on the other hand, spawn other affirming interactions and enable productive learning as students carry these feelings of security into the rest of their school day.

An essential part of ensuring school discipline, therefore, is taking deliberate measures to ensure a climate of friendliness and respect in hallways. This chapter discusses three top strategies for achieving this climate:

- Establish hallway rules and age-appropriate behavior expectations.

- Teach and practice hallway behaviors.

- Create orderly and friendly arrival and dismissal routines.

Establish Hallway Rules and Age-Appropriate Behavior Expectations

Schools often find it helpful to apply schoolwide rules to hallways (see Chapter 3). If your schoolwide rules are well framed, they should be meaningful to students of all ages and allow the crafting of specific corresponding behavior expectations that are developmentally appropriate for each grade. A "Be responsible" rule, for example, means we might expect all students to move quietly (not necessarily silently, which is developmentally inappropriate for children), keeping their hands and feet to themselves. But for kindergartners, "being responsible" may additionally mean that they must be with a teacher when they're in the hall.

Here's how you can bring your school to a shared understanding of these specific hallway behavior expectations.

Invite student input

It's important that we understand how students are feeling as they travel the school's hallways. So as a first step, you might ask teachers to talk with their classes about:

- Whether students feel safe in the hallways

- How students would like the hallways to sound and look

Students may or may not be spontaneously reporting social difficulties in the corridors, but with some honest classroom reflection and listening, we can learn a lot.

Discuss expected hallway behaviors at a staff meeting

At a staff meeting, have teachers share the student input from their classroom discussions. Then lead the group in arriving at a common understanding of what constitutes safe, friendly hallways at your school and how to achieve that vision. Following are some open-ended questions to guide this discussion.

What does safe hallway behavior look like and sound like?

- What behaviors should we be seeing if children and adults are following our school rules?

- How did students answer this question?

- How do their vision and ours compare?

How does current hallway behavior compare to these visions?

- What are students telling us?

- What are we observing ourselves?

What supports should we put in place to help children meet expectations and feel safe in the hallways?

Possible examples include:

- Having teachers make planned stops at corridor intersections when walking classes through the building

- Increasing teacher presence in the hallways during busy transition times such as arrival and dismissal

- Encouraging adults to use reinforcing language more often to support children's positive behavior

How should we interact with students traveling the hallways alone to run an errand for a teacher, go to the bathroom, and so forth?

- What should students carry? (A note from their teacher? A pass?)

- What do we say or do when we see a lone student without a note or pass?

- What about when we see a student *with* a note or pass?

- How should we interact with a child who's upset, perhaps crying, perhaps running?

- What consistent language, demeanor, procedures, and policies should we agree upon for these situations?

When staff have arrived at common answers to these questions, the school can take the next step of teaching students those hallway expectations and how to achieve them.

Teach and Practice Hallway Behaviors

As is true for recess and lunch, if we want children to behave safely and considerately in the hallways, we need to teach them how. The bulk of this teaching will be done by classroom teachers, but school leaders need to guide this teaching and to support it by giving students the same reminders, reinforcements, and redirections that their classroom teachers are giving them.

It's a good idea to give teachers a list of hallway behaviors to teach, perhaps also asking them to contribute ideas to the list. (See "Hallway Behaviors to Teach" on page 210 for a starter list.)

Then, share the following tips as you guide teachers in doing this teaching:

- **Clearly demonstrate how a routine or activity should look and sound.** It isn't enough to tell children to "walk quietly and with control." How quietly is "quietly"? What does "with control" mean? To clarify for students, encourage teachers to use interactive modeling, which lets children see and hear what their teacher is doing with her body and voice and then to practice the same actions themselves. (See Chapter 5 for details about interactive modeling.)

- **Keep expectations high but realistic.** It's important to consistently expect positive hallway behavior, but at the same time we need to make sure hallway expectations are realistic for children. For example, to prevent distracting classes in progress, we may institute a "walk silently in the hallways" rule, but walking silently is pretty much impossible for elementary aged students (it's even hard for many adults). So a policy of "walk quietly in the hallways" would be more realistic. Make sure that your school's policies are realistic and that teachers stick to them when teaching hallway expectations to their classes.

- **Break down the skills for young children.** Although older children may be able to practice a hallway trip from start to destination all at once, suggest that teachers of younger children break the practice into smaller chunks. For example, K–1 teacher Deborah Porter in Heath, Massachusetts, wanted to be able to walk behind the class line so she could see all the children and keep them safe while allowing them autonomy. She began by walking alongside the students, reminding them to be quiet with a gesture that she had taught them. Once that step was going smoothly, she positioned herself halfway down the hall and challenged the class to bring the line to where she was standing. Next, she moved a little farther down the hall, then all the way down the hall, and eventually out of sight (but to where she could still see them). Only when the class demonstrated that they could walk safely without seeing her did Ms. Porter take up her position at the end of the line.

■ **Role-play how to handle tricky hallway situations.** Any number of dilemmas can come up for students when they're in the hallway without their teacher. Laughter from the bathroom may beckon them to detour in to see what's going on. Or they may witness someone doing something mean to someone else and not know what to do. Encourage teachers to lead role-plays to help students develop a repertoire of positive ways to handle such situations (and occasionally go into classrooms to lead role-plays yourself). Teachers can ask students for situations to role-play. Their ideas can be eye-opening, providing a view of what hallways look and feel like to them. (To learn about role-playing, see *Rules in School: Teaching Discipline in the Responsive Classroom*, 2nd edition, 2011, available at www.responsiveclassroom.org.)

■ **Continue the teaching all year long.** Impress upon teachers that throughout the year, and especially around vacations and holidays, when children's self-control tends to diminish, they need to keep a close eye on students' hallway behavior, reteaching expectations through interactive modeling and role-playing as necessary. You should also continue your own vigilance and keep backing up teachers' efforts by giving students reminders and reinforcements of positive hallway behaviors.

HALLWAY BEHAVIORS TO TEACH

Here's a starter list of basic hallway behaviors to explicitly teach to students. You'll want to add others that are specific to your school. Clearly communicate the list to all teachers so that all students experience consistent teaching.

■ Walking quietly in line

■ Walking safely on stairs

■ Leaving an appropriate amount of space between people in line

■ Acknowledging others without being disruptive (teach young children to wink and wave to acknowledge friends rather than calling out; older students can give a gentle high-five or a wave)

■ Going directly from point A to point B (without any detours)

It's essential that all the adults in the school show these same behaviors in the hallways themselves. Make sure to establish this expectation early in the year for all staff members, including custodians and office staff, and to be a model yourself of appropriate hallway behavior.

Create Orderly and Friendly Arrival and Dismissal Routines

What's the morning arrival scene like at your school? What about afternoon dismissal? Do the children enter and leave the building in an orderly way? Do they get unruly in the hallways? Or are they relaxed and friendly toward one another?

Beginnings and endings are so important. Morning arrival can set the tone for the rest of the school day. Afternoon dismissal can determine students' (and adults') mindset as they leave school and affect whether they return the next day ready and eager for more learning. School leaders who invest time in creating an orderly and positive start and end to the day and who also provide sufficient transition times in the schedule find their investment repaid many times over in more productive student learning.

Each school must design its own arrival and dismissal routines to fit its situation. Here are just a few examples from schools that have transformed these times of their day.

A mini-assembly each morning

At Ideal Elementary, a K–6 school in Countryside, Illinois, arrival used to be chaotic. Students entered the building from several directions, depending on whether they arrived by bus, by car, or on foot. There was no designated place for early arrivers to wait. Students dawdled in the hallways and got rowdy before the morning bell.

After conversations and planning, principal Steve Bahn and a group of teacher leaders instituted the following arrival routine: First thing each morning, all students and staff would gather in the gym for a quick five- or six-minute assembly before the children went to their classrooms. Intended to build a sense of community schoolwide, the assembly would include a greeting, the pledge of allegiance, a lively activity (such as joke-telling on "Wacky Wednesdays"), and brief announcements.

Students were carefully taught every step of the new routine, and all school members—children and adults—were given time to practice it. "Staff members were amazed at what a difference this made in the tone of the day," recalls team member Alida Ressa. Students liked the new routine, too. One fifth grader says, "It helps me feel good in the morning, and it lets me know what to expect for the day."

If it's not practical at your school to start with an assembly, make sure there's a safe place for students who arrive early to go. Many schools have students gather in a central hallway or meeting space where they can read or talk quietly until the bell rings. Be sure this space is supervised and that there's an orderly procedure for dismissing students when the school day begins.

Adult hallway greeters at arrival

As at Ideal, morning arrival was unruly and potentially unsafe at Dame School, a preK–2 school in Concord, New Hampshire. Children would enter the building haphazardly and then talk loudly and run down the halls.

The school's first step was to have teachers deliberately teach students what safe, friendly hallway behavior looked and sounded like. The next was to have adults (teaching and nonteaching staff) present in the hallways in the morning to greet the children as they entered the building.

On a typical morning, the morning bell rings, and a moment later children start coming through the front door of the school. "Good morning, Parker," Linda Stephenson, the guidance counselor, says to a first grader as he passes by. Parker and all the other children pass and are greeted by several other adults on their way to their classrooms. They return the adults' greetings with a cheerful "Good morning!", a quiet nod, a quick hug, or a brief conversation about something that happened at home the night before. Besides calming and quieting the hallway scene, these brief noninstructional interactions show students that the adults care about them.

A few minutes after the children start entering the building, the flow of students diminishes to a trickle. Another bell sounds to start the day—a more peaceful and productive day than was typical in the past.

A warm, orderly send-off at dismissal

Four Corners Elementary School in Greenfield, Massachusetts, had one exit door and 229 students who needed to go through that door at the end of the day.

Multiple classes converged from two main hallways into a raucous bottleneck near the exit. As a result, dismissal time was tense and irritating for both the children and the adults.

Closing Circle

The end of the school day can be a hectic and anxiety-producing time. In addition to being tired, students often feel rushed, and some may feel worried about the afternoon's activities or their evening at home.

One idea for addressing this problem so that the day ends on a positive note is to encourage all teachers to hold a five- to ten-minute closing circle before dismissal. In the closing circle, students calmly celebrate their successes and look forward to the next school day. This manageable routine peacefully wraps up the day and sends students off feeling relaxed and accomplished, rather than anxious and rushed.

(For more on ending the day with calm closure, see "Closing Circle: A Simple, Joyful Way to End the Day" by Dana Januszka and Kristen Vincent, *Responsive Classroom Newsletter*, February 2011, available at www.responsiveclassroom.org.)

Instead of dismissing students to leave on their own, the school's solution was to have teachers walk their classes out of the building and to do so in a staggered fashion between 2:50 and 3:00. This solution ensured that only a few classes would be in the hallways at a time. At the spot where the two main hallways met, teachers would stop their lines, and classes would take turns exiting the building. The teacher of the exiting class would stand at the door and say a quick, personal goodbye to each student.

Besides easing the traffic congestion and sending the children off on a positive note, the new routine had a number of other benefits:

- When teachers negotiated the turn-taking where the two hallways met, they provided students with a model of courtesy and respect.

- For the classes waiting their turn to exit, the few minutes of wait-time gave teachers an opportunity to check in informally with students and for students to chat with each other and wave to friends in other classes. It was a casual but supervised and orderly social time.

- The routine provided an efficient way to keep track of each child at dismissal. As teachers said goodbye to each child, they would check off that child's name on a list. Principal Gail Healy could then check the lists and know when she could wave the buses to go.

SUCCESSFUL ARRIVAL AND DISMISSAL ROUTINES

- **Clarify the problem and your goal.** Be specific. Instead of "The hallways are chaotic," identify specific causes of the chaos, whether it's traffic congestion, children not knowing where to go, or some other issue. Name specific goals. For example, Ideal Elementary (see page 211) named two goals in improving the arrival scene: to create a more orderly and positive start to the day, and to build a schoolwide sense of pride and community. Those goals led to the idea of an assembly and helped dictate its format. The more specifically you identify the problem and goal, the more likely your solution will bring true improvement.

■ **Involve a key team in crafting solutions.** At Ideal Elementary, the principal brought the hallway problem to a small group of teacher leaders responsible for supporting positive student behavior. At Dame School (see pages 211–212), the problem was taken up by the school's leadership team, which consisted of administrators, teachers, support staff, members of the community, and parents. Decide who should be on your team and lead the team to work collaboratively to solve the problem.

■ **Have ample adult presence in hallways.** Nothing ensures safe, considerate hallway behavior more effectively than having adults there giving warm greet-ings, shaking hands or high-fiving, reminding children of hallway expectations or redirecting off-track behavior with a firm and respectful word or two, and reinforcing positive behavior with words and gestures.

■ **Anticipate staff concerns.** Before launching a proposed routine, think about concerns that staff might have (or solicit concerns from them). If you're thinking of instituting an early morning assembly, for example, staff might wonder how early arrivers will be supervised or what students are to do with their belongings during the assembly. Work out such details so the new routine will start off strong and earn wide enthusiasm.

■ **Think about whether students have the necessary foundational skills.** If you want students to give high-fives to say hello or goodbye, do they know how to do this gently and respectfully? If you want them to socialize quietly while wait-ing in line, do they know how to use "small voices" or "silent waves"? Have teach-ers teach these and all necessary foundational skills before launching the new routine.

■ **Give adults direction as needed.** Adults may need guidance in the new routine as well. For example, when Dame School began having adult hallway greeters, staff would clump up in certain spots in the hall, leaving other spots unsuper-vised. In response, the leadership team asked staff to stand at designated spots so they could even out the adult presence. ════════════════════

Reinforcing and Reflecting: Often Forgotten Steps in Teaching

Adults are pretty good about telling children what to do. But many of us forget two other crucial steps in teaching: giving children reinforcing feedback when they indeed do what we tell them to, and giving them opportunities to do their own reflecting on how they're doing in building new behaviors.

These two steps—reinforcing and reflecting—powerfully help children develop self-control. Rather than simply obeying external adult control, we want students ultimately to take responsibility for choosing appropriate behaviors themselves. Where I've seen children progressing to that stage in their growth, it's been because adults gave them reinforcing feedback and guidance in doing some reflective thinking about their behavior.

Reinforcing children's positive actions requires just a few brief words or a quick nonverbal gesture. Caltha Crowe, a third grade teacher, after seeing her students walking the hall in the safe, calm way she taught them, says to them, "Even though it was really hard, almost everyone was doing quiet waves to their friends. You were keeping your bodies in control. You were walking quietly." When she reinforces desired behaviors like this, the children are more likely to keep behaving in those ways. (See page 52 in Chapter 4 for more on reinforcing language.)

Reflections can be just as brief. Ms. Crowe often builds them into the normal flow of activity. One day early in the year, when the children are still getting the hang of walking quietly and calmly in the hall, she stops the class on their way to the auditorium and has them do to a quick self-check. "Thumbs up, in the middle, or down for how you're doing walking quietly and with your bodies in control." All the children put their thumbs up. "OK, go ahead." The class proceeds.

Such self-checks take no more than a minute, yet they effectively help children stay conscious of their behavior and help consolidate their learning.

Be There Yourself

No one's presence in hallways is more pivotal than the school leader's, especially during arrival and dismissal. We don't need to be there every day at both times—that would be impossible—but we do need to be present often enough to send a message. Our presence tells staff, students, and parents that the hallway space is important to the school leader. It tells them that we care enough about having safe, orderly, and friendly hallways to take time out of our busy days to personally help make that a reality.

Buses

SCHOOL LEADER'S CHECKLIST

❑ **Establish meaningful bus rules**

❑ **Help students get to know their bus drivers**

❑ **Teach and practice bus behaviors.** Involve:

    ❑ Bus drivers

    ❑ Bus supervisors

    ❑ Classroom teachers

❑ **Create procedures for responding to and reporting problems**

❑ **Problem-solve with bus riders and bus drivers**

❑ **Consider older-grade bus buddy weeks**

❑ **Help students find positive bus activities**

❑ **End the day with bus rehearsal**

CHAPTER 15

Buses

Ensure a safe ride to and from school

For the twenty-four million children in the U.S. who ride buses to school, the school day begins and ends on the bus. For these children, what happens on the bus—whether these yellow transports are "friend ships" or bullying incubators—can set the entire tone of school.

Children spend a lot of time on buses: a thirty-minute ride each way translates to 180 hours per year per child, the equivalent of 25.5 full days of school. That's a lot of learning time. But what do students learn during all these hours? On the one hand, children are stretched toward autonomy: They choose whom to sit with, decide what they will talk about, figure out what to say or do when there's a problem—all important life skills. On the other hand, for too many children on too many rides, the lessons learned on the bus are difficult and painful ones about teasing, taunting, and bullying. Clearly, addressing bus behavior has to be an integral part of any school's efforts to improve discipline.

This, admittedly, can feel like complicated, daunting work. Many school leaders, frankly, are stymied about what to do about bus behavior problems besides reprimanding students, calling parents, or handing out warning slips and bus suspensions. Some of us have tried more intensive solutions such as bus monitors, closed circuit TV monitors, and school suspensions, only to find that these usually don't result in long-term improvements in student conduct. Others among us believe that nothing works, that bus misbehavior is one of those facts of childhood that can't be escaped.

But there *are* remedies that bring significant and sustainable change—remedies that use positive methods to teach and support children in choosing expected behaviors. This chapter discusses the following strategies:

- Establish meaningful bus rules.

- Help students get to know their bus drivers.

- Teach and practice bus behaviors.

- Stay in touch with bus riders.

- Create procedures for responding to and reporting bus problems.

- Consider older-grade bus buddy weeks.

- Help students find positive bus activities.

- End the day with bus rehearsal.

Establish Meaningful Bus Rules

A first step toward safe and orderly bus behavior is establishing meaningful bus rules, and that begins—as with rule creation for any area of school—with developing a shared vision of what positive bus behavior looks and sounds like. This envisioning and rule establishing can be done by just the adults at school or by both the adults and students. (See Chapter 3 for more on rule creation.)

An example that involves students

Grafton Elementary, a grade 3–5 school in Grafton, Massachusetts, provides an example of bus rule creation that involved students. At Grafton, all 700-plus students ride the bus. "That means fifteen buses with all the usual problems, including bullying," says fifth grade teacher Martha Hanley. Recognizing that children's experiences on the bus were affecting their ability to learn in school, she and a group of other teachers decided to work with the children to make their bus rides a safer and more pleasant time.

They began with bus rule creation. The teachers divided up the buses among themselves—two buses per teacher. Each teacher then arranged a twenty-minute rule creation meeting with her bus riders early in the school year. At these meetings, the children, who spanned the school's three grades, got to know one another and shared ideas about what good days on the bus were like. Following an adaptation of the *Responsive Classroom* rule-creation process that the school was using for classroom rule creation, each bus group then produced a short, general list of rules that would ensure more good bus days.

Even though each bus ended up with slightly different rules, all the groups covered similar ideas about being safe, respectful, and kind to others. Because the children were also still expected to follow the "Bus Riders' Code of Conduct" in the student/parent handbook, the teacher helped them understand how the code's requirements, such as "Sit down when the bus is moving," fit with their own rules about being safe and respectful.

Engaging students in bus rule creation, the school found, helped the students feel more invested. As Ms. Hanley says, "Having rules for their bus in their own words made those rules more meaningful." The school then used the rules as the basis for all further work with students on bus behavior.

Help Students Get to Know Their Bus Drivers

As educators, we know how important a strong teacher-student relationship is to children's developing positive behavior in the classroom. A similar principle applies to the bus. If we can help children form positive relationships with their bus drivers, their behavior on the bus can only improve. Here's how two schools orchestrated this relationship-building between bus riders and bus drivers.

Brayton Elementary: interviews of bus drivers. When teachers at Brayton Elementary School in North Adams, Massachusetts, decided to address their school's bus problems, they began by asking the children for ideas. Why do so many children "go bananas" on the bus, they asked in brainstorming sessions. The children's answer was surprising in its wisdom: because they didn't know their bus drivers.

"Kids realized that they don't act this way in class because they know their teacher. What if they were to know their bus driver?" says third grade teacher Karen Lefave.

With this cue from the students, the teachers at Brayton organized the children to do get-to-know-you interviews of their bus drivers. The children made posters using information from their interviews and photos of the drivers and then hung the posters throughout the school. "Meet the driver of the Flower Bus," said one poster. "His name is Mr. Wilson. He has a dog. He likes to travel." An extra bonus of this project was that the displays helped all school members see the bus drivers as part of the school community.

South Hill Elementary: Q&A sessions between drivers and riders
South Hill Elementary School in Ithaca, New York, took a slightly different approach. As part of a broader effort to address bus behavior, the principal organized Q&A sessions between each bus driver and his or her riders. The children asked about their driver's hobbies, family, even favorite color.

Then the whole group went outside, where children took a close look at their buses' safety features. The conversation then turned to what it's like to drive a bus and how important it is that the children are calm and quiet on the bus so the driver can concentrate on driving.

Crafting your own approach

These are just two ways to help students get to know bus drivers. You'll need to lead your school in crafting your own approach and decide who should facilitate the effort (school leaders, specialists, counselor, or teachers) and whether activities ought to be done bus by bus or class by class.

Whichever approach you take, be sure to provide staff time for the project as well as encouragement and problem-solving support. Your leadership is key to ensuring that this is a meaningful experience for all involved and to showing both the adults and children that your school is serious about improving bus discipline.

Teach and Practice Bus Behaviors

Just as we take time to teach children what it looks and sounds like to follow classroom, recess, lunch, and hallway rules, we need to do the same with bus rules. These demonstrations clarify for children exactly what's expected of them on the bus and why such behaviors are important. Teaching the behaviors also conveys to children that the bus is part of school and that the adults at school care about bus behaviors as much as behaviors anywhere else in school.

School leaders and classroom teachers both have important roles to play in teaching bus behaviors. The more we get positive bus behaviors on students' radar screen, and the more specific we are about what expected behaviors look and sound like, the more successful the children will be. Here are some strategies for making the teaching of bus behaviors consistent and of high quality at your school.

- **Launch the teaching yourself.** Doing so conveys to students that positive bus behavior is a high priority for the school. To help make the expected behaviors clear to students, model them right on the bus. Many schools are required to do bus evacuation drills with students at the beginning of the year. The time you block out for this teaching provides a great opportunity to also teach your school's day-to-day bus behavior expectations in the presence of the bus driver and any bus supervisors so that they, too, are clear about the school's behavior expectations.

- **Encourage classroom teachers to continue the teaching.** In their classrooms, teachers can also teach and reinforce expectations for positive bus behavior. To support them in this teaching, discuss bus discipline at a staff meeting so that all teachers have a shared understanding of specific behaviors that everyone will teach (see "Bus Behaviors to Teach" on page 224). Consider also setting up a pretend bus (chairs lined up in two rows) in the gym or cafeteria where this teaching can happen during the early weeks of school.

- **Use interactive modeling.** This simple technique (see Chapter 5 for details) works well for teaching walking safely down the bus aisle, getting the driver's attention safely, and other important bus behaviors. Be sure to use it whether you're teaching bus behaviors in an actual bus, a pretend bus, or a classroom.

- **Use role-playing.** This method of preparing children to handle complex social situations is perfect for bus dilemmas, which so often demand that students size up the situation quickly and choose from a range of possible responses. Encourage teachers to role-play bus dilemmas with their students, and go into classrooms to do role-play sessions yourself. (For information on role-playing, see *Rules in School: Teaching Discipline in the Responsive Classroom*, 2nd edition, 2011, available at www.responsiveclassroom.org.)

- **Use morning meeting time.** Suggest that teachers use some meeting time to reinforce positive bus behaviors. For example, if they use a *Responsive Classroom* Morning Meeting, the morning message can ask students to check off specific positive bus behaviors they observed that morning, such as children playing guessing games, sharing trivia cards, or sitting with a new friend. Or suggest that teachers look for opportunities at other times of the day to guide children in complimenting each other on kind and friendly acts on the bus.

- **Reinforce friendly bus conduct during all-school meetings.** Do quick, short, interactive modeling sessions of expected bus conduct at these schoolwide gatherings, focusing on a different behavior at each gathering.

- **Regularly put bus behavior on staff meeting agendas.** For example, use ten minutes of staff meeting time every other month to have teachers share how their teaching of bus behavior is going, name problems, and list possible solutions.

BUS BEHAVIORS TO TEACH

Here are some key routines and procedures to model and practice with students. Share this list with all teachers to ensure that all children benefit from consistent teaching and reinforcement of these behaviors.

- How to get on and off the bus

- How to walk down the aisle

- How to select a seat

- How to sit on the bus

- What to do while riding (appropriate voice level, travel activities, etc.)

- How to get the driver's or supervisor's attention

Stay in Touch With Bus Riders

Staying in touch with students who ride buses, continuously seeing how things are going on the bus, and staying in touch with bus drivers as well is one of the best ways to maintain bus discipline.

At Grafton Elementary, the Massachusetts school where a group of classroom teachers engaged students in creating rules for their buses (see pages 220–221), the teachers created a structure to ensure this tuning in rather than leaving it to chance: After creating bus rules with students, each teacher stayed in her "bus teacher" role throughout the year. They checked in with the riders of their buses from time to time and met with their riders at mid-year to revisit and revise the rules the group had created together. The school also had a system for students to put a note in their bus teacher's mailbox or speak with that teacher during the school's daily ten-minute morning break if they were having trouble on the bus.

The bus teachers also checked in with their drivers periodically to see how things were going from the driver's point of view. If there was a problem, the bus teachers would problem-solve with the riders and drivers and bring the issue to school leaders' attention if needed.

After this structure was up and running, bus incident reports dropped, problems were resolved more quickly, and the children's ability to concentrate in their classrooms improved.

If you create a similar program at your school, make sure it's sustainable. Have enough bus teachers so that each oversees only a few buses. Also provide time in the school schedule for bus teachers to meet with students and with each other about bus issues. (See "A Practice Bus for Real Problem-Solving" on page 227 for another way to keep in touch with students' bus lives.)

Create Procedures for Responding to and Reporting Bus Problems

Most bus companies have protocols for bus drivers to follow if children are not following safety rules (such as asking a child to move to the front of the bus where she can be more closely supervised). In addition to these standard procedures, it's important that schools establish their own protocols for how to handle behavior problems on the bus. Here are important steps in this work.

Make sure drivers know your school's expectations for bus behavior

This first step can be done by including the bus driver (and any other adults who ride the bus) in the modeling sessions as noted earlier. Or you can simply inform these adults of what student behaviors the school expects.

Assign adults as bus greeters

Make sure there are always staff members greeting the buses when they arrive at school. One of the greeters' jobs is to ask the bus driver if there were any behavior problems during the previous afternoon's or the current morning's ride. If there was a small problem, the greeter can hold the involved student on the bus and have a three-way conversation between student, bus driver, and greeter about the incident (or a four-way conversation if there is a bus supervisor). Frequently this quick check-in and a reminder about what to do in the future is all that's needed to resolve the issue.

Having bus greeters is also a proactive discipline strategy. Just knowing that there will be a greeter asking the driver about the ride right when the bus pulls up is often enough to improve most children's bus behavior. Also, if a child is having trouble during the ride, knowing that a staff member will be there when the bus door opens will be a source of comfort and likely help that child make it through the ride more calmly. Equally important, a warm, friendly hello from a supportive adult helps set a positive tone for the day for all children coming off the bus, especially on days when the bus ride didn't go well.

Create a form for easy reporting of significant bus problems

Bus drivers, supervisors, and greeters need an easy way to report behavior problems. One method that works well is to create a form to be completed whenever there's a problem that couldn't be resolved by the brief conversation conducted by the bus greeter. The form should provide a place to note the child's name and a list of problems that can be checked off—for example, "child didn't stay in seat," "child was yelling," "child was playing with window," and so forth.

Make sure the greeters always give the forms to the same person

In most schools, the principal or assistant principal is the appropriate person to receive bus discipline forms. Once you've designated the person at your school, make sure the forms always go to that person so that he or she can identify any patterns of behavior and respond accordingly.

CHIP REFLECTS

A Practice Bus for Real Problem-Solving

The moments after buses unload in the morning are a great time to do some teaching about bus behavior. Whatever happened that morning on the bus—good or bad—is fresh on the children's minds. Why not take a few minutes then to reflect with them, debrief, and do some real problem-solving?

This was the strategy I introduced at a small K–8 school in Massachusetts years ago when I was the principal there. In that rural town, many children had to ride the bus for up to forty-five minutes in each direction, more than enough time for bus problems to erupt.

I used chairs to set up a "practice bus" in the cafeteria. Each day, I took one busload of children there while students from other buses went on to their day as usual. We'd talk about that morning's ride. If it was a nice ride, we talked about what made it nice. How did students talk? What words and tone of voice did they use? How did they sit in the seats? The children demonstrated, using the practice bus. This conscious reflection reinforced for the children not only the importance of behaving positively, but *how* to behave positively.

If the morning's ride wasn't so nice, we'd talk about what made it not nice. Here I carefully guided the conversation toward constructive comments and away from finger-pointing. If necessary, we problem-solved or role-played. (If there was a fight or other conflict involving just a few students, I separately addressed it with them.) Debriefing about problematic rides in this way not only gave the children ideas for making future rides go better but also gave them time to cool down. Without this buffer, upset children would have taken their upset directly into the classroom, a sure recipe for disruption and reduced learning. (For an example of solving bus conflicts, see Appendix C of *Solving Thorny Behavior Problems: How Teachers and Students Can Work Together* by Caltha Crowe, 2009, available from www.responsiveclassroom.org.)

Mornings are, of course, the busiest time of day for principals. When you have announcements to make and parents to see and breakfast to cover, it's hard to stop to deal with a busload of children.

So if you want to try this at your own school, share the load. Have school counselors, interventionists, and other appropriate personnel take turns doing the morning bus program. Teach these staff the job of the debriefing leader. Emphasize that the leader's most important task is to create the space, spirit, and energy for practicing positive bus behavior.

Finally, don't forget to publicly recognize the "nice" bus behaviors that students report. (Recognize the whole bus; don't single out individuals.) You can send a note to all classes: "Students on Bus Four said it was friendly on their bus because kids said hello, used calm voices, stayed in their seats, and kept their hands and feet in their own spaces." Teachers or students can then read the note aloud in each classroom.

Consider Older-Grade Bus Buddy Weeks

Do older bus riders sometimes bother the younger ones at your school? You can try turning this around by designating certain weeks when older and younger students will be paired as bus buddies and then teaching the older students to look after their younger charges. Children's behavior often shifts dramatically when they're given real responsibility to help others, especially those younger than themselves. Not only that, but having bus buddy weeks reinforces the message that at this school, we take care of one another.

Consider the following if you want to establish bus buddies:

- **Try it *before* there are problems**. Try it for a week on one bus as a pilot. Have children report their experiences at all-school gatherings or to their classes. Then see if other buses would like to give it a try. Or establish buddies on all buses the week of the fall Open House and discuss with parents what their children are reporting about their bus rides.

- **Have a "bus buddy invitation" procedure.** Establish a way for younger children to write an invitation and deliver it to a potential bus buddy in an older class. (In this scenario, not everyone would have to have a bus buddy, and buddies wouldn't have to pair up every day.)

- **Ask teachers to talk about bus buddies in morning meeting.** Teachers can spend a day or two in morning meeting having the children come up with ideas for how bus buddies should behave toward each other and what they might do together on the bus.

Help Students Find Positive Bus Activities

Drawing, doing homework, reading, and folding origami are just a few calm, quiet activities that we can guide children to do on the bus. Travel games that reinforce skills they're working on in school are another good bet. *Who can spot the most license plates from out of state? Which state's license plate is the most common after our home state's? What signs of the seasons do you see out the bus windows? How many animals can you spot?* You can even hold friendly competitions among buses or have buses create posters of their sightings for display in the hallways. The possibilities are many—invite staff and the students themselves to come up with ideas.

To support positive activities on the school bus:

- **Keep two clipboards, paper, and a pencil on each bus.** Assign student leaders to keep track of these supplies and use them for bus games and contests.

- **Teach travel games.** Suggest that teachers encourage parents to send in favorite family travel games. Better yet, teachers can invite parents in to teach the games to the class.

■ **Encourage children to try classroom games on the bus.** Many morning meeting activities and classroom energizers can be adapted into travel games. Suggest that teachers help children create such adaptations.

End the Day With Bus Rehearsal

The end of the day is a great time for teachers to rehearse the upcoming bus ride with children. "All bus riders, I'd like to see you at the meeting area for five minutes. The rest of you can read your library books quietly at your tables," a teacher might say. With the riders gathered in a circle, the teacher can then quickly review the bus rules or teach the children a new travel game to play during the upcoming ride.

The end of the day is also the time for teachers to privately rehearse a bus ride with individual students who may need some extra support. "Bus calls will start in ten minutes, Jeremy. What quiet activity will you do on your ride home today?"

Of course, to do these rehearsals, teachers need to stop teaching ten minutes before buses are called. But that's good teaching practice anyway. One of the best ways to preserve teaching quality and student achievement is to stop teaching early enough so that after cleanup, packup, and homework reminders, there's time for a calm closing circle to reflect and end the day on a positive note.

Many teachers will find it tough to stop teaching ten minutes early, given the pressure they feel to squeeze maximum content coverage into every minute of the school day. That's where we school leaders come in. We need to set a tone of "do less to achieve more" by explicitly encouraging teachers to schedule this ten-minute end-of-day closure.

Reflection is so important to students' development of positive habits. Bus rides—and other aspects of school—will go more smoothly if we give children time to reflect. (For more on ending the day with calm closure, see "Closing Circle" on page 212 and "Closing Circle: A Simple, Joyful Way to End the Day" by Dana Januszka and Kristen Vincent, *Responsive Classroom Newsletter*, February 2011, available at www.responsiveclassroom.org.)

The Most Instructive Social Interaction

Experienced educators know that the greatest learning occurs through social interaction. Social interaction is as instructive on the school bus as in the classroom. But exactly what will children learn in this mobile classroom? The answer depends on whether school leaders prioritize the bus as an important part of the school day and the teaching of bus behaviors as a critical piece of the school curriculum.

Schoolwide Rule Creation

A landmark in a 14-month journey
to improve school climate

by Kevin White and Chip Wood

From the *Responsive Classroom® Newsletter*, November 2005

Sheffield Elementary, a grade 3–6 school in Turners Falls, Massachusetts, faced a challenge familiar to many educators: how to develop a more consistent approach to discipline from classroom to classroom and in common school areas, such as the playground, lunchroom, and hallways.

In the fall of 2003, our school community had identified ensuring a positive school climate as a top priority. We wanted to devise consistent, schoolwide disciplinary policies to help children follow school rules. These policies would apply to all behavior, whether occurring within or beyond the classroom. Next, we needed to help the children create the schoolwide rules. Then we had to help them learn what following those rules would look like, feel like, and sound like. What, for example, does a common rule such as "Be kind" look, feel, and sound like for children sharing the lunchroom space?

All of these steps were integral to improving the school climate. The step that this article focuses on is the creation of the schoolwide rules, undertaken in fall 2004, the second year of our project. Students, parents, teachers, counselor, and principal worked hard together to create a Sheffield "Constitution"— a set of schoolwide behavioral guidelines distilled from separate sets of classroom rules. As our second year progressed, we began to see some positive results: Our use of common teacher and student language about behavior and rules, the emphasis on teacher modeling, and a great deal of practice in living our constitution all helped make the school climate more peaceful and productive.

Schools will find many ways to do the hard work of developing school-wide rules, depending on the ages and needs of their students. Here is what the process looked like at Sheffield.

Are We Ready?

We began our work formally in January 2004. We adults (principal, counselor, teachers, support staff, and parents) asked ourselves two key questions about our readiness to help the children formulate and follow schoolwide rules:

1. Did we have a clear set of disciplinary policies that let everyone know how to help children who had trouble following the rules?

2. Did the children know how to formulate and follow rules in their own classrooms?

Disciplinary policies: In place before school started

In January 2004, a task force made up of teachers, other staff, and parents began exploring what a schoolwide discipline plan would look like. The task force set up discussions with the entire staff and surveyed parents, staff, and the whole student body (over 270 students). They received written responses from 243 students, 104 parents, and 43 out of 55 staff. The active involvement of so many members of the school community was important, given the size and complexity of the project.

One outcome of the discussions was the creation of a set of disciplinary guidelines for handling children's behavior problems anywhere in the school. The guidelines were eventually included in the parent-student school hand-book, which we sent home with students in September of the 2004/05 school year. These guidelines included three "Steps to Self-Control" that would help children get their behavior back on track when they were having trouble following classroom or schoolwide rules:

1. When children begin to lose control, teachers remind them of the rules and, if necessary, calmly and concisely redirect their actions. For example, to a child disrupting another student's work, a teacher might say "Take your work to that table, Brady."

2. If children continually choose to ignore the rules or are so upset that they cannot follow the rules, they need a few minutes in a safe place

to cool down. This "Take-A-Break" area is within the children's classroom. Sometimes a buddy teacher's classroom is used as a next step.

3. If children continue acting out, they need to spend more time in a quiet place. In our Peace Room, an adult helps upset students interrupt a pattern of nonproductive behavior. Students stay in the Peace Room until they show their readiness to be welcomed back into the classroom.

The parent-student handbook also explained that teachers and staff adapt these steps for use in the lunchroom, hallways, and other school spaces. For example, a child who is becoming too noisy at lunch may be told to go for a calming-down break in the Peace Room, which is right across the hall. The handbook also let parents know that any nearby adult member of the school community will take responsibility for guiding children through these steps to self-control.

The handbook goes on to discuss that when these steps are not enough, we may keep students after school for social skills tutoring with the principal. We also let parents know that we still use suspension (either in or out of school, depending upon child and family needs) for serious misconduct.

Classroom rules: Created

At the start of the 2004/05 school year, each class had created their own classroom rules. In schools like Sheffield, where teachers use the *Responsive Classroom* approach, teachers work with the children to create the classroom rules. Generated from students' ideas, these rules set limits in a way that fosters group ownership and self-discipline. Teachers find over and over that this investment of time and effort is well worth the payoff of calm, productive, and joyful classrooms. Classroom rule creation takes place in the early weeks of school. Here is what the process typically looks like.

1. **Articulating hopes and dreams**

   The teacher helps students set goals for the year, often beginning by sharing her or his own goals.

2. **Generating rules**

   Teacher and students collaborate to generate rules that allow all class members to achieve their hopes and dreams.

3. Framing the rules in the positive

The teacher works with students to turn rules about what not to do into ones about what to do. For example, "Don't run" might become "Move safely."

4. Condensing the list

The teacher helps students consolidate their long list of specific rules into three to five broad classroom rules. Students make a poster of the rules and display it prominently in the room.

By late September, the classes at Sheffield had been learning and living with their rules for several weeks.

Creating Our Constitution

At the end of September 2004, after fourteen months of working hard together, we had classroom rules and a set of clear disciplinary policies in place. Finally, we were ready for the children to create their schoolwide rules—the Sheffield Constitution.

To enhance academic learning as the children worked on their schoolwide rules, we decided to guide them through the same sort of democratic process that resulted in the creation of the U.S. Constitution in 1787. In the classrooms, teachers noted that our school's process for making schoolwide rules would be similar to the one by which our nation's founders had created the most important laws of our country. The steps were as follows:

The grade-level mini-convention

Each of the school's fourteen classes chose two delegates to represent them at a grade-level mini-convention. The job of the delegates at each grade-level mini-convention was to discuss all the classroom rules for their grade and select three to five upon which all could agree. We felt that as an important part of the students' learning, they should have some say in how they would arrive at their grade-level rules, as long as their method was fair and respectful. Some delegates voted rule by rule for inclusion or exclusion. Others grouped similar rules so that they could more easily decide among them. One grade felt it important to include at least one rule from each classroom.

The mini-convention delegates talked about what the words they were using meant—words such as "respect" and "responsibility." One group of students said that respect meant "listen when the teacher's talking; don't talk back." Another group said that respect meant "be nice to everybody." Students also discussed what it would look, sound, and feel like to follow the rules they were crafting. "If Raina were being kind to Maria when Maria's looking for a lunch seat," the adults asked, "what might she say or do?" One student said, "She could say, 'Maria, you can sit at our table.'" Another student suggested that Raina could wave to get Maria's attention and point to the empty spot at her table.

By the end of the mini-convention, we had four sets of three to five rules, one set for each of the grades in our school. We were ready for the next step.

On to the Constitutional Convention

Before adjourning, the classroom delegates decided which two delegates would represent their whole grade at the Sheffield Constitutional Convention. On September 27, 2004, these eight grade-level delegates, along with the school counselor and principal, set off for "Philadelphia"—the superintendent's conference room on the other side of our complex. After a formal greeting and words of encouragement from superintendent Sue Gee, the delegates got down to the business of transforming four sets of grade-level rules (a total of approximately sixteen rules) into one set of three to five schoolwide rules.

Taking their responsibility quite seriously, the delegates reviewed and discussed and struggled to find a way to reduce the many rules down to just three to five. They tried choosing rules from the various class posters. They tried categorizing and grouping rules that were similar. We (their principal and counselor, the only adults present) offered suggestions and gentle guidance. But the first hour passed and the delegates had not agreed on a single rule.

At this point, we offered the delegates a challenge: We would leave the room and return in five to ten minutes. The delegates' task: Agree on the most important rule and write it on the chart paper. We checked in at the end of five minutes and were told "Not yet!" We were worried: Would this work? Was the task too big? Would the children be able to come up with even that first rule? After another ten nerve-wracking minutes, we were welcomed back into the room. There on the paper was one word in big, bold letters: ENJOY!

The delegates were excited. We adults were pleasantly surprised by the concise and powerful first rule. But we were still worried: Would the children finish the rest of the rule-making successfully? We were politely told to "go away again." The students would work on the second rule and tell us when they were ready. We waited in the hall. Each time we checked, we were told "Not yet!" As school dismissal approached, we began to wonder if the task could be completed on time.

Finally, we were signaled back in. Expecting to see only rule two added below rule one, we were delighted to see instead five rules and a very satisfied-looking group of delegates. After about an hour and a half of serious deliberation, fourteen sets of rules crafted by over 270 students were now represented by one set of proposed schoolwide rules:

Enjoy!

Respect everyone and everything around you.

Speak kindly.

Be helpful and responsible.

Take care of classrooms and school property.

The delegates were now ready to present their work to the school community.

The rules ratification ceremony

On October 6, 2004, the whole student body assembled in the auditorium along with teachers, parents, principal, counselor, and official guests. All the rules from which the schoolwide rules had been distilled—the fourteen classroom rules posters and the four sets of grade-level rules—were displayed at the front of the auditorium.

Mr. White, the school counselor, asked all the students, teachers, and other school staff to stand. "Everyone you see standing here," he said, "participated in creating the classroom rules that are the foundation for the schoolwide rules we will ratify today." The whole auditorium rang with enthusiastic applause. Mr. White then heightened the excitement by asking everyone to be seated except for the two delegates from each of the fourteen classrooms. Of these twenty-eight children, eight (the grade-level delegates) were sitting on the stage. After another big round of applause, Mr. White asked all these students, except for the eight on the stage, to be seated. He then turned everyone's attention to the stage, where the eight sat with the superintendent of schools, school committee chair, fire and police chiefs, town select board, and other local officials. Behind them hung a giant poster of the Sheffield Rules, which had been commercially produced to emphasize the importance of the occasion.

Mr. White described the long and careful process these eight delegates had followed to distill the schoolwide rules from so many sets of classroom rules. Then he invited the delegates to explain each schoolwide rule. "Rule one," they said. "Enjoy. That means enjoy learning, enjoy your classmates, enjoy your teachers, enjoy recess, enjoy school." In similar fashion, they explained each of the remaining four rules. When they finished, the rules were affirmed by voice vote and a stirring standing ovation. Invited guests congratulated the delegates on their accomplishment. The guests also reminded all of the students that for the work they had done to be meaningful, the whole school community (children and adults) would need to help one another learn and live by the constitution in the months ahead.

Posting and distributing copies of the constitution

After the ratification ceremony, smaller versions of the Sheffield Rules poster were given to staff for posting in classrooms and in the hallways, lunchroom, library, and other common school areas. In the classrooms, teachers helped children see how the Sheffield Rules were similar to their own classrooms rules. For example, a teacher might say, "The Sheffield Rules are the ones we follow when we're outside our classroom. They have the same ideas as our classroom rules, although some of the words are different." The teacher might then guide the children through a comparison of words and ideas to help them relate the two sets of rules.

Parents also received copies of the schoolwide rules with reminders of which pages in the parent-student school handbook would apply when any of these rules was broken.

Moving Into the Future

Creating schoolwide rules and disciplinary policies helped Sheffield School take a huge step toward resolving concerns about school climate. Engaging all of the children in the rule-setting process helped them take ownership of the rules. Engaging all of the adults emphasized for the children the significance of their work. Together, we are creating a calmer, happier place for learning.

We know our schoolwide rules need to belong not just to the students present in our constitutional year, but to all the students following them. That means discussion, modeling, and practice of the rules as we welcome new children each year. It also means ongoing communication among all the adults of the school community. Sharing insights and observations is the best way to know if the rules are helping us meet our hopes and dreams for all the children.

Colleague Consultations

Six steps to understanding and solving problem behaviors

This appendix outlines a brief process that school adults can use for consulting with colleagues to understand children's problematic behavior and strategize a response. The process can be used for problems involving one child or multiple children.

Teachers can use the process to address behaviors they're seeing in their classrooms. Nonclassroom staff or a small blended group of teachers and nonteachers can also use this process to address behaviors in shared spaces such as the hallways, playground, lunchroom, and bus. For example, if a school is having recurring issues with lunch routines and behaviors, a school leader may ask the cafeteria staff to join with other school adults to explore the problem through this process. If hallway behavior is the issue, a school leader may invite a small group of teachers and administrators to use this process to bring the issue before colleagues.

The Six Steps

1. Get ready for the consultation by observing the child's behavior over time.

2. Gather a group of colleagues and designate a facilitator.

3. Describe the child and the problem.

4. Invite clarifying questions.

5. Listen to problem-solving strategies that colleagues suggest.

6. End the session.

Following is a description of what this process looks like when a teacher uses it to consult with colleagues about a student's problematic behavior in her class.

Step 1: Getting ready

The teacher takes time to carefully observe and take notes on the child's behavior over time. The goal is to be able to clearly and factually articulate the problem. For an additional perspective, teachers might invite a colleague to observe as well. While observing, it's helpful for teachers to ask themselves the following questions:

- What are some of the child's strengths, interests, and positive behaviors?

- What is the child's developmental age and where does this fit with other children in the class?

- What specific behavior is problematic?

- What background information (learning style, past school experiences, family information, etc.) do I have about this child?

- What is the environment in which the behavior occurs?

- What happens just before and after the behavior?

- What is the frequency of the behavior? Is this something that has been occurring all year? At what time of day does it occur?

- What are other children doing when this behavior is occurring? How does this behavior affect other children? How does it affect me?

- What positive strategies have I tried? What kind of success have I experienced with these strategies?

- How have I responded to the behavior? What language have I used? How have I gone about stopping the behavior?

Step 2: Gathering a small group of colleagues

The teacher gathers together a group of colleagues who are willing to help. The group chooses someone to be a facilitator. It also establishes or reaffirms group norms, which typically include maintaining confidentiality (participants will not bring up the issue outside of the meeting), maintaining a nonblaming and nonjudgmental attitude, and adhering to the time limits and steps of this consultation process.

Step 3: Describing the child and the problem (3–5 minutes)

The teacher spends up to five minutes describing the student and the specific problem (based on the observation she did prior to this meeting and her answers to the reflection questions listed above). The teacher presents this information objectively to maintain empathy for the child or children and to characterize the behavior, not the child or children, as the problem. Issues of confidentiality may require that names not be used.

Facilitator's job: Keep track of time.

Step 4: Inviting clarifying questions (5–10 minutes)

Going around the circle, colleagues ask the teacher questions to better understand the child and the problem. It's most helpful to use open-ended questions. For example:

- "Can you describe this child's connection with other students?"

- "Can you tell us more about this child's positive participation at other times of the day?"

- "What have you learned about this child's behavior outside your classroom (during PE, lunch, recess, music, etc.)?"

The teacher may either respond to the questions asked or write down the questions and think about them later. The goal here is for the teacher to present as detailed a picture of the problem behavior as possible.

Facilitator's job: Structure the process so that everyone has an opportunity to ask a question or pass. Redirect the group if they offer suggestions or ask "Have you tried . . . ?" questions that are actually suggestions.

Step 5: Listening to possible problem-solving strategies

The facilitator checks with the teacher to see if the steps taken so far are sufficient. Sometimes the process of presenting the problem and considering colleagues' clarifying questions is enough to deepen a teacher's understanding of the problem. In that case, the teacher thanks the group for their help and closes the meeting.

If the teacher wants suggestions for how to handle the problem, the facilitator invites the group to brainstorm problem-solving strategies. The teacher now assumes the role of listener and takes written (or mental) notes of ideas generated by colleagues. These will likely include ideas that the teacher has already tried. It is not necessary for the teacher to say "I've already tried that." Instead, she listens and takes in what's helpful. If needed, she may ask clarifying questions following a suggestion.

Examples of suggestions that colleagues might offer:

- "You might want to consider using more interactive modeling prior to the times of day when the child experiences the most problems."

- "Sometimes proximity or a gentle hand on the shoulder might help provide a calm reminder."

- "Limiting children's choices might help."

- "Providing more reinforcing language when the child is exhibiting positive behaviors might strengthen the teacher-student relationship."

- "Providing written rubrics or directions for activities might help the child better know what's expected."

- "Consider engaging the child in a problem-solving conference at another time of day."

- "Communicate with the family to find out how they deal with this behavior at home."

- "Consider having the child take a break in a buddy teacher classroom when the behavior becomes disruptive."

Facilitator's job: Structure the process so that all group members have an opportunity to offer a suggestion or pass. Keep the process focused by reminding the teacher not to say "I tried that but . . ." and reminding the group that this is not a time for discussion.

Step 6: Ending the session

The facilitator checks with the teacher to see if more information is needed. If not, the meeting ends. The goal of conferencing with colleagues in this way is to help the teacher better understand a problem and leave with strategies that she may choose to try; the teacher need not share what she plans to try. The facilitator reminds everyone that once the session is over, it is over. Participants agree not to bring up the issue with each other or initiate conversation about it with the teacher unless she invites them to do so.

Tapping Into Collective Intelligence

Often our ability to solve a problem is directly related to our ability to describe it. In this powerful consultation practice, colleagues use their collective experience and expertise to help a teacher describe a problem accurately and thoroughly. They also generate possible solutions that the teacher may not think of alone. As an added benefit, often the ideas generated find relevance with other teachers in the group, who may be struggling with similar issues themselves.

A Repertoire of Conversation Formats

Learning-focused conversations among the adults at school are vital to building better discipline. Through these conversations, staff members clarify what they know, gain new knowledge, and devise promising problem-solving strategies.

When facilitating these conversations, school leaders need to shape the discussion so that participants feel respected and engaged. One way to do this is to provide conversation formats that match the purposes of the conversations. Here are formats you might try, grouped by two common purposes of staff discussions. Rotate through different formats as much as possible to keep discussions fresh and to tap into different strengths in staff members.

Purpose: Talking to Understand

- **Sharings.** You could do an around-the-circle sharing in which each person responds to a topic or question you pose to the whole group. Or you could do a partner share in which partners listen to and then paraphrase each other's ideas for the whole group.

- **Jigsaws.** These are ideal for discussing readings. Individuals are assigned to read different sections of a text (section A, section B, section C, and section D, for instance). Those who read section A get together to form an "expert group" on section A, those who read section B form an expert group on section B, and so forth. Each expert group discusses its section of the text and agrees on key ideas from that section. Participants then shuffle and form "jigsaws groups" made up of one representative from each expert group (each jigsaw group has a section A expert, a section B expert, a section C expert, and a section D expert). In the jigsaw groups, each expert shares the important ideas from her section of the text and takes questions and comments from the group.

■ **Written conversations.** Staff form small groups. Each person responds in writing to a question (for example, "What teacher behaviors—yours or others'—are helping children meet hallway expectations?"). After two minutes of free writing, participants pass their paper to the right within their groups, read the previous person's comment, and add to it.

■ **Give one/take one.** Participants independently generate ideas related to an issue or problem (for example, strategies they've used or want to use to support children's positive behaviors in the cafeteria). They mingle, trading one idea with a colleague (sharing one idea and collecting one) before moving on to another colleague.

■ **Plusses and challenges.** Divide a large sheet of chart paper into two columns. Label one column "Plusses" and the other "Challenges." Name an issue (for example, children's bus behavior). The group brainstorms plusses (practices and structures that are helping children behave positively) and challenges (practices and structures that are contributing to children's misbehavior). Record or have someone record all ideas on the chart. The group then chooses one or two of the challenges to work on.

Purpose: Talking to Generate Solutions to Problems

■ **Brainstorming and consolidating.** Pose a question (for example, "How can we make dismissal time calmer and friendlier so that everyone, whether student or adult, ends the day on a positive note?") The group brainstorms while you or someone else records everyone's ideas and then sorts the ideas into broad categories. Participants then form small groups, one for each category. Each small group crafts a statement that captures all the specific solutions named in their category.

■ **Circle map.** Divide staff into small groups and give each group a sheet of chart paper. Announce a topic (for example, "How to improve our use of reinforcing language"). Each group draws a big circle on their paper and writes the topic in the middle of the circle. Group members brainstorm ideas related to the topic and write them randomly around the paper within the circle, without attempting to organize the ideas. After awhile, groups exchange papers and categorize the ideas on the sheet they received, marking each category with a different colored marker and giving each category a name (for example, "Observe" or "Be specific"). Then the charts are returned to the original groups for review and reflection.

■ **Narrowing choices.** When the group needs to narrow down a long list of possible solutions, try these strategies:

  ◆ Plusses and minuses—Participants identify advantages and disadvantages of each idea.

  ◆ Unlivable only—Participants identify choices they can't live with and explain why.

  ◆ Livable only—Participants identify ideas they can live with (as many as they'd like).

  ◆ One why—Participants identify the one idea they prefer and explain why.

  ◆ Three straws—Participants name their top three choices.

■ **Carousel charts.** This is a great method for identifying common threads in related discipline topics—for example, skills children need if they're to be successful (a) in the hallway (b) in the lunchroom (c) on the playground and (d) on the bus. Staff form small groups, one for each subtopic, and brainstorm ideas, recording them on a chart. Groups then rotate to read one another's charts, adding ideas or circling common themes. The whole group then reflects on common themes.

■ **Concentric circles.** Participants form two concentric circles, the inside circle turned out so that each person stands facing a partner. Partners discuss possible solutions to a problem you pose (for example, "What can we do differently to improve student behavior at recess?"). After a couple of minutes, people in the outer circle take a step to the left so that everyone has a new partner. Continue with the same or a related question. After a few rounds, the group shares big ideas and identifies common themes.

Recommended Resources

The strategies in this book will be even more effective if teachers in your school are using the *Responsive Classroom®* approach to teaching. To learn about that approach, see the following resources, all of which are available from www.responsiveclassroom.org.

Foundation-Setting During the First Weeks of School: Taking time during the critical first weeks of school to establish expectations, routines, a sense of community, and a positive classroom tone:

> *The First Six Weeks of School* by Paula Denton and Roxann Kriete. 2000.
>
> *Guided Discovery in a Responsive Classroom* DVD. 2010.
>
> *Teaching Children to Care: Classroom Management for Ethical and Academic Growth K–8*, revised ed., by Ruth Sidney Charney. 2002.

Rule Creation and Logical Consequences: Helping students create classroom rules to ensure an environment that allows all class members to meet their learning goals; responding to rule-breaking in a way that respects students and restores positive behavior:

> *Creating Rules with Students in a Responsive Classroom* DVD. 2007.
>
> *Rules in School: Teaching Discipline in the Responsive Classroom*, 2nd ed., by Kathryn Brady, Mary Beth Forton, and Deborah Porter. 2011.
>
> *Teaching Discipline in the Classroom* Professional Development Kit. 2011.

Preventing Bullying at School: Using practical strategies throughout the day to create a safe, kind environment in which bullying is far less likely to take root:

> *How to Bullyproof Your Classroom* by Caltha Crowe. 2012. Includes bullying prevention lesson plans.

Solving Behavior Problems With Children: Engaging children in solving their behavior problems so they feel safe, challenged, and invested in changing:

> *Solving Thorny Behavior Problems: How Teachers and Students Can Work Together* by Caltha Crowe. 2009.

> *Sammy and His Behavior Problems: Stories and Strategies from a Teacher's Year* by Caltha Crowe. 2010. (Also available as an audiobook.)

Positive Teacher Language: Using words and tone as a tool to promote children's active learning, sense of community, and self-discipline:

> *The Power of Our Words: Teacher Language That Helps Children Learn* by Paula Denton, EdD. 2007.

> *Teacher Language in a Responsive Classroom* DVD. 2009.

> *Teacher Language* Professional Development Kit. 2010.

Interactive Modeling: Teaching children to notice and internalize expected behaviors through a unique modeling technique:

> *Interactive Modeling: A Powerful Tool for Teaching Children* by Margaret Berry Wilson. 2012.

> *Rules in School: Teaching Discipline in the Responsive Classroom*, 2nd ed., by Kathryn Brady, Mary Beth Forton, and Deborah Porter. 2011.

> *Teaching Children to Care: Classroom Management for Ethical and Academic Growth K–8*, revised ed., by Ruth Sidney Charney. 2002.

Working with Families: Hearing parents' insights and helping them understand the school's teaching approaches:

> *Parents & Teachers Working Together* by Carol Davis and Alice Yang. 2005.

Barros, R., Silver, E., & Stein, R. (2009). School Recess and Group Classroom Behavior. *Pediatrics*, 123 (2): 431–436.

Bill Summary and Status, 11th Congress (2009–2010). H.R. 4223. Retrieved November 2, 2010, from Library of Congress THOMAS: http://thomas.loc.gov/cgi-bin/bdquery/z?d111:h.r.04223:.

Bodrova, E., & Leong, D. (1995). *Tools of the Mind: A Vygotskian Approach to Early Childhood Education*. Upper Saddle River, New Jersey: Prentice Hall.

Bryk, A., & Schneider, B. (2002). *Trust in Schools: A Core Resource for Improvement*. New York: Russell Sage Foundation Publications.

Bryk, A., Sebring, P. B., Allensworth, E., Luppescu, S., & Easton, J. Q. (2010). *Organizing Schools for Improvement: Lessons from Chicago*. Chicago: University of Chicago Press.

Collaborative for Academic, Social, and Emotional Learning. (2008). *Connecting social and emotional learning with mental health*. Washington, DC: National Center for Mental Health Promotion and Youth Violence Prevention, Education Development Center. Retrieved October 27, 2010, from http://www.casel.org/downloads/SELandMH.pdf.

Delisio, E. (2005, January 18). Recess Before Lunch Can Mean Happier, Healthier Kids. *Education World*. Retrieved March 18, 2009, from http://www.educationworld.com/a_admin/admin/admin389.shtml.

Delpit, Lisa. (2006). *Other People's Children: Cultural Conflict in the Classroom*. New York: New Press.

Denton, P. (2007). *The Power of Our Words: Teacher Language That Helps Children Learn*. Turners Falls, Massachusetts: Northeast Foundation for Children.

Garmston, R. J., & Wellman, B. M. (2008). *The Adaptive School: A Sourcebook for Developing Collaborative Groups*. Christopher-Gordon Publishers, Inc.

Garmston, R. J. (2005, Spring). Create a Culture of Inquiry and Develop Productive Groups. *Journal of Staff Development*, 26 (2): 65–66.

Ginott, H. (1972). *Teacher and Child: A Book for Parents and Teachers.* New York: Scribner Book Company.

Ginsberg, K. (2007). The Importance of Play in Promoting Healthy Development and Maintaining Strong Parent-Child Bonds. *Pediatrics*, 119 (1): 182–191.

Guskey, T. R. (2002). Professional Development and Teacher Change. *Teachers and Teaching: Theory and Practice*, 8 (3/4): 381–391.

Illinois Learning Standards, Social/Emotional Learning (SEL) Resources. (2006, July 18). *Frequently Asked Questions (FAQs) about social and emotional learning (SEL)*. Retrieved October 27, 2000, from the Illinois State Board of Education website: http://www.isbe.state.il.us/ils/social_emotional/pdf/sel_learning_faq.pdf.

Jarrett, O. S. (2003). Recess in Elementary School: What Does the Research Say? Retrieved February 20, 2009, from ERICDigests.org. http://www.ericdigests.org/2003-2/recess.html.

Knowles, M., Holton, E. F., and Swanson, R. A. (2005). *The Adult Learner: The Definitive Classic in Adult Education and Human Resource Development.* Portsmouth, NH: Heinemann.

Latest policy developments. (n.d.). Retrieved October 26, 2010, from CASEL website: http://www.casel.org/standards/print.php?url=standards/policy.php.

Lawrence-Lightfoot, S. (2003). *The Essential Conversation: What Parents and Teachers Can Learn from Each Other.* New York: Random House.

Leonard, G. B. (2000). *The Way of Aikido: Life Lessons from an American Sensei.* New York: Plume.

Montana Office of Public Instruction. (2009). Recess Before Lunch Policy: Kids Play and Then Eat! Retrieved March 18, 2009, from http://www.opi.state.mt.us/schoolfood/recessBL.html.

National Coalition for Parent Involvement in Education. (2006, January). *Research Review and Resources*. Retrieved September 23, 2010, from http://www.ncpie.org/WhatsHappening/researchJanuary2006.cfm.

National review of state SEL learning standards. (n.d.). Retrieved October 26, 2010, from http://www.casel.org/standards/print.php?url=standards/learning.php.

Palmer, P. (1999). *The Courage to Teach: Exploring the Inner Landscape of a Teacher's Life*. Hoboken, New Jersey: Wiley.

Pastor, P. N., Reuben, C. A., and Loeb, M. (2009). Functional Difficulties Among School-Aged Children: United States, 2001–2007. *National Health Statistics Reports*, Centers for Disease Control and Prevention, U.S. Department of Health and Human Services. Number 19, November 4, 2009.

Piercy, M. (1980). *The moon is always female*, 1st ed. New York: Knopf.

Regulations Establishing Standards for Accrediting Public Schools in Virginia, 8 VAC 20-131 (2006).

Rimm-Kaufman, S. E. (2006). *Social and Academic Learning Study on the Contribution of the* Responsive Classroom® *Approach*. Turners Falls, Massachusetts: Northeast Foundation for Children.

Siegel, D. (2007). *The Mindful Brain: Reflection and Attunement in the Cultivation of Well-Being*. New York: W.W. Norton and Company.

U.S. Department of Agriculture, Team Nutrition. (2000). Changing the Scene: Improving the School Nutrition Environment. Retrieved December 7, 2010, from http://teamnutrition.usda.gov/Resources/guide.pdf.

U.S. Department of Education, Office of Planning, Evaluation and Policy Development. (2010, March). *ESEA Blueprint for Reform*. Retrieved October 27, 2010, from http://www2.ed.gov/policy/elsec/leg/blueprint/blueprint.pdf.

Wenner, M. (2009, January). The Serious Need for Play. *Scientific American*. Retrieved March 19, 2009, from http://www.sciam.com/article.cfm?id=the-serious-need-for-play.

Wyoming Department of Education. (n.d.). *Eat Smart, Play Hard Wyoming! Benefits of Recess Before Lunch Fact Sheet*. Retrieved March 15, 2010, from http://www.laramie1.org/modules/groups/homepagefiles/cms/120925/File/Nutrition/recess.pdf?sessionid=ca.

Acknowledgments From Chip Wood

The seeds for this book were planted thirty years ago when a kindergarten teacher, a special education teacher, a high school and community college educator, and an elementary principal began a school and a nonprofit educational foundation with a shared vision about the way school could be. In the K–8 laboratory school founded by Marlynn Clayton, Ruth Charney, Jay Lord, and me, we put into practice the ideas and ideals about teaching and learning we considered most critical to children's physical, cognitive, social, and ethical development. These practices would result later in the creation of the *Responsive Classroom* approach. Principal among our early colleagues were Roxann Kriete and Mary Beth Forton, who, today, continue to skillfully guide the work of Northeast Foundation for Children (NEFC) and the expansion of the *Responsive Classroom* approach to more and more elementary schools nationwide—Roxann as executive director and Mary Beth as director of communications and publications.

I am especially indebted to Roxann Kriete, whose support and encouragement continue to mean so much, for her astute organizational leadership and most especially for her steadfast friendship and shared vision of educational excellence.

The practices at the heart of the *Responsive Classroom* and its approach to classroom and school discipline were brilliantly articulated by Ruth Charney in her seminal book *Teaching Children to Care: Classroom Management for Ethical and Academic Growth, K–8*, first published in 1991. Thousands of teachers and school leaders have deepened their understanding of children's behavior and improved their approaches to classroom and school discipline by reading this book, myself included. I am grateful to Ruth for her concrete approaches and remain ever thankful for her steadfast, passionate commitment to the principles of nonviolence. Today, when addressing the issue of bullying is on the minds of all educators, we would do well to listen to Ruth's words: "No school advocates the use of violence, but few would define nonviolence as a core curriculum. I envision schools actively engaged in a curriculum of nonviolence."

It has been my privilege to have worked on such a "lived curriculum" with teachers and school leaders in schools across the country for twenty-three years as part of NEFC and, more recently, as principal of Sheffield Elementary School in Turners Falls, Massachusetts. I want to thank all my colleagues in the Gill-Montague Regional School District, particularly Sherry Wood, Kevin White, Annmarie Hallowell, Betsy Burnham, Carrie Burke, Dr. Christine Jutres, Elizabeth Musgrave, and Superintendents Carl Ladd, Ken Rocke, and Sue Gee, who fully supported implementation of the *Responsive Classroom* approach. Leadership counts in matters of discipline.

I am deeply grateful to all who have taught me about school and personal discipline over the years, especially Sheila Kelly, Deborah Porter, Kathy Brady, Linda Crawford, Terrance Kwame-Ross, Rachael Kessler, Maurice Sykes, Caltha Crowe, Marion Finer, Paula Denton, Tina Valentine, Parker Palmer, Rick and Marcy Jackson, and Pamela Seigle.

Thanks, at NEFC, to Babs Freeman-Loftis, co-author of this book, for her remarkable insights. Also to Gretchen Bukowick, Karen Casto, Elizabeth Nash, Mike Fleck, Danielle Letourneau-Therrien, Allison Henry, Mike Anderson, and so many others for their collaboration and support over the years. Love to my wife, Reenie; my children, Jonathan and Heather; my grandchildren, Isaiah and Lily; and all the schoolchildren who have provided much instruction these past forty years.

Finally, my very special thanks to Alice Yang, book editor at NEFC, without whom my writing would truly be incomplete.

Acknowledgments From Babs Freeman-Loftis

I am indebted to the many colleagues, administrators, parents, and children who have walked the path of education with me during my long tenure at University School of Nashville and my work with Northeast Foundation for Children. I am a better teacher, parent, friend, colleague, and author because of them.

My professional relationship and personal friendship with former administrator and mentor Kathy Woods have been a pivotal and grounding influence throughout my teaching career, not to exclude work on this project. I want to thank Paula Denton for leading me to this work with the *Responsive Classroom* approach, and for inspiring much of the thinking that helped to shape many of the ideas in this book. My steadfast friend and colleague Margaret Wilson provided encouragement and support along the way, and Roxann Kriete and fellow teammates Mike Anderson, Kerry O'Grady, Karen Casto, Tina Valentine, and Andy Dousis generously shared ideas and group thinking as we were exploring this topic of school discipline. It has been an honor to work on this project with Chip Wood. The inspiration and vision that Northeast Foundation for Children's co-founders Chip, Marlynn Clayton, Jay Lord, and Ruth Charney brought to the educational landscape in the early 1980s changed the way that I and thousands of other teachers view teaching. Ruth Charney writes in her book *Habits of Goodness*, "As teachers share more with each other they, too, gather the courage of their convictions." All these people have afforded me with innumerable opportunities to gather the courage of my convictions.

I have learned so much about collaboration and partnership from Alice Yang, our editor. She is masterful at articulating the big ideas and hopes for a project and at providing the perfect balance of support and space.

I learned from Mom and Dad that balancing firmness and kindness was indeed the best recipe for managing large groups of children (they had plenty of practice). My husband, Tom, understands as no one else how important this work is to me and finds a way to infuse a large measure of humor and balance into my life. Our children, Matthew, Maggie, and Nathan, and Nathan's wife, Erin, provide us with a large dose of inspiration and joy. I have loved the hours of conversation with my daughter Maggie about discipline. Her work in the therapeutic field has challenged me to think about the wide range of needs that children and families face.

I spoke with dozens of school leaders and teachers throughout the writing of this book. Special thanks go to Beth Thornburg, Barb Snyder, Matt Miller, Stephanie Bisson, Tim Kasik, Lisa Kostaneski, Cindy Kruse, Rose Monterosso, Marty Kennedy, Peter Anderson, Jeremy Abarno, Kathy Brady, Cheryl Ollman, Rita White, Wendee Beller, Amy Berfield, Courtney Fox, Jeff Greenfield, and my sister and personal writing coach/cheerleader, Beth Moore. My hopes are that this book will validate what schools believe about how to best reach and teach all children with dignity, respect, and kindness and that it provides the practical strategies and inspiration needed to help others gather the courage of their convictions.

The authors would like to thank manuscript readers Dennis Copeland and Rita White for their valuable feedback. The authors are also grateful to the Northeast Foundation for Children publishing team, including Helen Merena, designer; Elizabeth Nash, copyeditor; and Mary Beth Forton, director of communications and publications. The talents and hard work of all these people were indispensible to the successful completion of this book.

Chip Wood has been an elementary school teacher, principal, district curriculum director, and teacher educator during his forty-year career in education. In 1981, Chip co-founded Northeast Foundation for Children, developer of the *Responsive Classroom* approach to teaching. Chip is the author of *Yardsticks: Children in the Classroom Ages 4–14* and *Time to Teach, Time to Learn: Changing the Pace of School*. He is also a facilitator for the Center for Courage and Renewal, which offers reflective retreats and professional development experiences for teachers and school leaders based on the work of Parker J. Palmer. Chip lives with his wife, Reenie, and their daughter, Heather, and her two children in Massachusetts.

Babs Freeman-Loftis taught elementary physical education for fourteen years before moving into administration as an assistant principal for nine years. Babs began using the *Responsive Classroom* approach in 1998. She now provides coaching and consultations to schools and districts using the approach. Babs also presents and helps develop *Responsive Classroom* workshops for administrators and teachers. She is a co-author of *The Responsive Classroom Assessment Tool for Teachers*. She lives with her husband, Tom, in Nashville, Tennessee.

═══════ A B O U T   T H E   P U B L I S H E R ═══════

Northeast Foundation for Children, Inc., a not-for-profit educational organization, is the developer of the *Responsive Classroom®* approach to teaching. We offer the following for elementary school educators:

Publications and Resources

- Books, CDs, and DVDs for teachers and school leaders

- Professional development kits for school-based study

- Website with extensive library of free articles: www.responsiveclassroom.org

- Free quarterly newsletter for elementary educators

- The *Responsive®* blog, with news, ideas, and advice from and for elementary educators

Professional Development Services

- Introductory one-day workshops for teachers and administrators

- Week-long institutes offered nationwide each summer and on-site at schools

- Follow-up workshops and on-site consulting services to support implementation

- Development of teacher leaders to support schoolwide implementation

- Resources for site-based study

- National conference for administrators and teacher leaders

For details, contact:

Responsive Classroom®

Northeast Foundation for Children, Inc.
85 Avenue A, Suite 204, P.O. Box 718
Turners Falls, Massachusetts 01376-0718

800-360-6332 ■ www.responsiveclassroom.org
info@responsiveclassroom.org